VOICES
OF
SOUTH
AFRICA

BOOKS BY CAROLYN MEYER

Nonfiction

THE MYSTERY OF THE ANCIENT MAYA
WITH CHARLES GALLENKAMP

AMISH PEOPLE:
Plain Living in a Complex World

THE CENTER:
From a Troubled Past to a New Life

THE BREAD BOOK:
All About Bread and How to Make It

MASK MAGIC

Fiction

ELLIOTT & WIN

C. C. POINDEXTER

EULALIA'S ISLAND

THE SUMMER I LEARNED ABOUT LIFE

THE LUCK OF TEXAS MCCOY

VOICES OF SOUTH AFRICA

▼▼▼▼▼▼▼▼▼▼▼▼

GROWING · UP · IN A · TROUBLED · LAND

◄◄◄◄◄◄◄◄◄◄◄◄

BY CAROLYN MEYER

GULLIVER BOOKS

HARCOURT BRACE JOVANOVICH

SAN DIEGO AUSTIN ORLANDO

Requests for permission to make copies of any
part of the work should be mailed to:
Permissions, Harcourt Brace Jovanovich, Publishers,
Orlando, Florida 32887.

Library of Congress Cataloging-in-Publication Data
Meyer, Carolyn.
    Voices of South Africa.
    "Gulliver books."
    Bibliography: p.
    Includes index.
    Summary: The author recounts her visit to South
Africa where she interviewed numerous young people,
both black and white, to find out what growing up is
like in a country torn apart by racial strife.
    1. Youth—South Africa—Social conditions.
2. Youth—South Africa—Attitudes. 3. Apartheid—
South Africa. [1. South Africa—Social conditions.
2. Blacks—South Africa. 3. Apartheid—South Africa]
I. Title.
HQ799.S5M49   1986   305.2'35'0968   86-45059
ISBN 0-15-200637-0

Designed by Julie Durrell

Printed in the United States of America
First edition
A B C D E

968

For Margaret K. McElderry

CONTENTS

vii

CONTENTS

CONTENTS

Map appears on pages x–xi

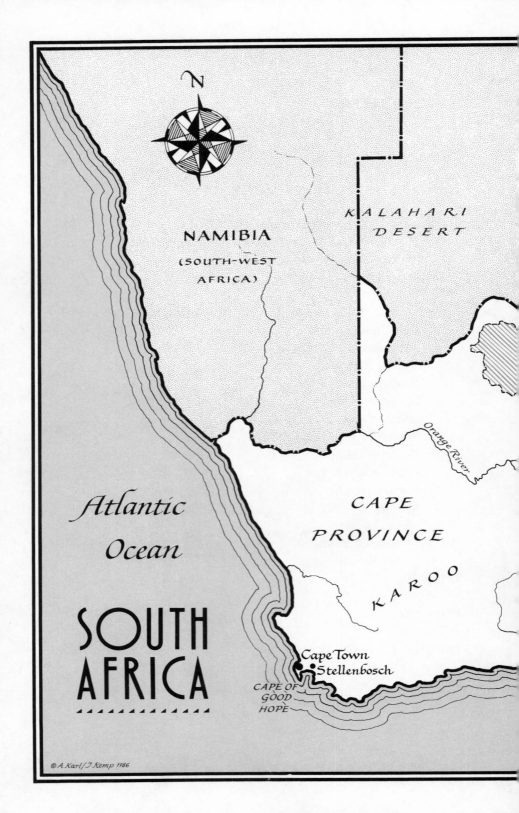

N

NAMIBIA

(SOUTH-WEST
AFRICA)

KALAHARI
DESERT

Orange River

CAPE

PROVINCE

KAROO

Atlantic

Ocean

SOUTH
AFRICA

Cape Town
Stellenbosch

CAPE OF
GOOD
HOPE

© A. Karl / J. Kemp 1986

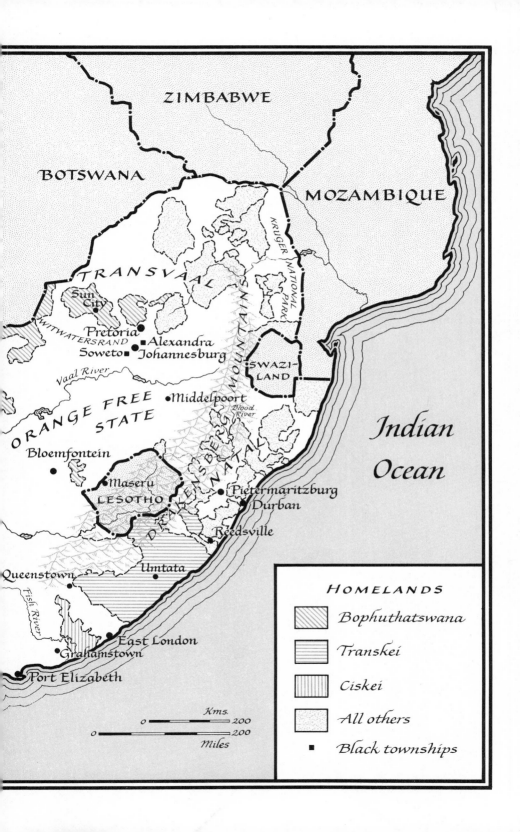

ZIMBABWE

BOTSWANA

MOZAMBIQUE

T R A N S V A A L

KRUGER NATIONAL PARK

Sun City

WITWATERSRAND

Pretoria
Soweto■ ■Alexandra
Johannesburg

SWAZI-
LAND

Vaal River

ORANGE FREE
STATE

Middelpoort

Blood River

DRAKENSBERG MOUNTAINS

NATAL

Bloemfontein

Maseru
LESOTHO

Pietermaritzburg
Durban

Reedsville

Queenstown

Umtata

Indian

Ocean

Fish River

East London
Grahamstown

Port Elizabeth

Kms.
0   200
0   200
Miles

HOMELANDS

Bophuthatswana

Transkei

Ciskei

All others

■ Black townships

PART ONE

The Cape of Good Hope

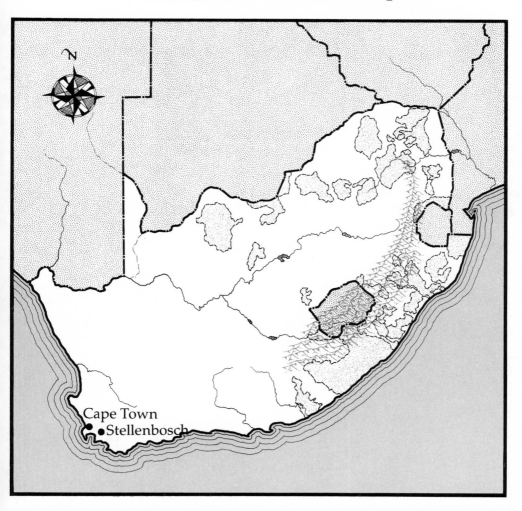

PROLOGUE
LANGA

Samuel Mkunqwana

▲▲▲▲▲ **T**he classrooms were empty, the school deserted except for a handful of students and a skeleton staff of teachers. Samuel sat behind a desk in the Language Arts room and tried to explain to me why he was boycotting this school in Langa, a Black township near Cape Town. St. Jerome's, a Roman Catholic high school, was designated by the South African government to tutor Black students who had not yet managed to pass their final year.

"The idea," Samuel said patiently, "is not to boycott the *school* but to boycott the *classes*."

He has been trying to persuade his classmates to show up for "alternate instruction." They would be taught non-White history—the Freedom Charter, for instance, drawn up by the African National Congress in the 1950s—instead of the other kind of instruction.

Other kind of instruction?

3

"The educational system for Blacks in this country is a tool designed by Whites to keep us in our place. We've had enough of that. By not teaching us well, by not letting us know what we need to know, they keep us powerless. They say that we 'learn differently,' that we are not capable of learning what White people do, or of learning it the way they do. I don't think they really believe that. But they know very well what would happen if they allowed us to have educations like theirs!"

Black students may have had enough, but Samuel was painfully disappointed in the results of the boycott. Instead of gathering at the school for the alternate instruction in a show of solidarity, students were simply staying away. That accomplished the closing of the school but not much else. Some tried to study at home with telephone help from sympathetic White teachers. Samuel had never had much luck with home study.

Bright and articulate, Samuel Mkunqwana (pronounced, roughly, mm-kun-KWAH-nah) is twenty-two years old. His slow academic pace is clearly not due to lack of brains or ability. Samuel blames a number of factors; one is his home life. After his mother died a few years ago, he went to live with his grandmother and a variety of aunts and cousins packed into a six-room house, a total of thirteen people that climbed to seventeen on weekends. There is never any place to study, never any quiet when four or five people always seem to be in the same room, talking. Besides that, Samuel has to share his textbooks with three other students. It takes money for uniforms (required in all schools), transportation, school supplies. It has been necessary for him to drop out from time to time to go to work. Always he comes back, but his dream of becoming a mechanical engineer slips farther away, probably forever beyond reach.

Two more students stopped by the classroom to see what was going on. Timothy, whose goals of dismantling the ed-

4

ucational system sounded less ambitious than Samuel's, described the boycott as a way of putting pressure on the South African government to lift the state of emergency that had been in effect for several weeks. He hopes to become a medical technologist, probably as much out of the question as Samuel's ambition. Mamphela, a tiny girl with close-cropped hair, wants to study physiotherapy. She is one of ten children—"There isn't even enough love to go around, let alone enough money"—and she is abandoning her plans.

What do you do for *fun*? I asked them, veering away from the inadequate education, the lack of money, the frustration. All three of them stared at me, as though I had asked a totally irrelevant question. Timothy shrugged and said he sometimes plays soccer; Mamphela occasionally goes to the flicks (South Africans have a number of words for movies—flicks, cinema, bioscope). Samuel has a girlfriend, but he rarely sees her. Is she involved in the struggle, too? He shook his head and said firmly, "I don't want that."

Timothy and Mamphela drifted out again. Samuel and I looked at each other across the bare desk. He wore a faded green plaid shirt and a small moustache. "Why do you trust me enough to talk to me so openly?" I asked him.

"It's a decision I made," he said. "I say what I think is right."

"That could get you into trouble."

Samuel smiled faintly. "I know."

The earnest young red-haired principal of St. Jerome's paced in front of the inspirational poster on his office wall. The poster showed a figure in silhouette gazing out upon a sweeping vista of purple mountains streaked with an orange sunset. The message flowed in script below the figure: "You see things as they are and ask 'Why?' But I dream things that never were and ask 'Why not?'"

5

The principal was frustrated by the boycott too, but for different reasons. "These students are in their twenties, they haven't passed their exams, and yet they want university degrees and the prosperity that represents," he said. "Nobody wants to go to a technical school, nobody wants to be a plumber or an electrician. They're hopelessly unrealistic about their chances, because they don't properly assess their academic abilities. They don't understand how far behind they are, or what it would take to catch up."

Samuel wants to be an engineer, not a plumber.

I pointed to the poster. "On the one hand you encourage them to dream, and on the other you tell them their dreams are foolish."

The principal blushed to the roots of his sunset-colored hair.

South Africa has been making headlines for a long time. Whenever violence erupts between Blacks and Whites on the other side of the globe—and it often does—it is reported by American newspapers and television. Several incidents stand out.

The Sharpeville Massacre on March 21, 1960, began as a peaceful demonstration against the pass laws, a requirement that every Black South African over the age of sixteen carry a passbook stating where that person may live and work. But the demonstration ended in the death of 67 people and the wounding of 186, including 40 women and 8 children. Many of the dead and wounded were shot in the back, fleeing from the police. The violent turmoil that followed the shootings prompted the government to clamp down hard, declaring a state of emergency which permitted the police to arrest whom they chose without warrant and to detain them indefinitely without charges. Thousands of people were arrested and held in prison for months.

The next date burned into Black memory is June 16, 1976, when twenty thousand students in Soweto, the gigantic Black township adjacent to Johannesburg with a population estimated to be between a million and a half and well over two million, protested educational policies. Hundreds were killed.

That protest—and the killings—spread to the Cape, the largest of South Africa's four provinces, extending from the Atlantic Ocean on the west to the Indian Ocean on the south and east and then north to the borders of South-West Africa (Namibia) and Botswana, with the violence concentrated in the cities. Since 1976 school boycotts in the Cape have come and gone, but violence—Blacks against White institutions and, more recently, Black mobs against Black individuals—has increased steadily. Furious Blacks, who have no vote and little money, struggle to wrest power and prosperity from Whites whom they outnumber five to one; Whites resist in an attempt to retain the privilege and wealth they have acquired since their arrival in South Africa over three centuries ago.

In the summer of 1985 headlines in black and white again crackled on the front pages of newspapers around the world. Schools were shut down by stone-throwing Black students. White policemen leaped out of armored vehicles and waded into the crowds wielding leather whips called sjamboks (pronounced SHAM-boks), firing rubber bullets, and lobbing canisters of tear gas. Once again the South African government slapped on repressive measures, declaring a state of emergency in various parts of the country, the first since Sharpeville. Police hauled thousands of people off to jail to be detained for however long it pleased the authorities—some say as many as nine thousand people in 1985. The number of deaths, almost always Blacks, mounted daily. The world reacted with outrage.

But the South African government and many White citizens responded angrily, telling the world, in effect, to mind its own business. They reminded the United States of its own far-from-perfect record in race relations, of its treatment of Blacks and "Red Indians," as they call Native Americans. Meanwhile, the U.S. Congress debated whether or not to impose economic sanctions, measures designed to put pressure on the South African economy so that the government would be forced to change its repressive, inhumane tactics.

For years America has insisted that South Africa eliminate apartheid (pronounced ah-PAR-tate, a word meaning "separateness"), the philosophy of racial segregation reinforced by an elaborate system of powerful laws that gives a minority of about 4.5 million Whites total control over a huge majority of approximately 20.7 million Blacks and 3.4 million other non-Whites. Basic to apartheid is a system of racial classification that labels every South African at birth and determines how and where that person may live and work from that moment on. Despite my own dislike for pigeonholing people, I will use the South African government's classifications in this book: White, Coloured, Asian, and Black (referring to Black Africans), though frequently "Black" is used to refer to everyone who is not lucky enough to have been born with a white skin.

For years South Africa responded to criticism with token gestures—such as permitting a few "international" hotels and restaurants where Blacks are admitted as well as Whites, and allowing Blacks long-term leases on their homes rather than restricting them to renting. But in the summer of 1985, gestures were no longer enough. The country seemed destined to erupt from a combination of internal and external pressures. Young Black South Africans were angry, terribly angry, and they were focusing much of their fury and their frustration on the very thing that middle-class Whites (and many middle-class Blacks as well) insist should help them: their schools.

In the midst of this, I decided to go to South Africa.

Not just because I had heard of its beauty: its rugged mountains and beautiful coast. Not just because I had read about fascinating game preserves where elephants topple trees, curious giraffes peer over high branches, and graceful impala leap for the sheer joy of it. Not just because I had been told that South Africans—*White* South Africans—are among the friendliest, most hospitable people in the world (to other Whites). And not because I am a voyeur of violence.

I went because I wanted to find out what it was like to be a young person growing up in such a place at such a time, when minority Whites have so much to lose and majority Blacks—in some ways as different from each other as they are from Whites—have so little to lose that their own lives have ceased to hold much value.

I wanted to cover as much territory as possible in the time I had, staying with families when I could arrange it, visiting schools when I could find one that was open or that would let me in, and striking up conversations with strangers wherever I went.

I rode taxis and trains and planes and got people to drive me around. Eventually I rented a car and took off on my own, getting used to driving English-style on the left side of the road, converting kilometers to miles, liters to gallons, South African rands to dollars. I made mistakes. Sometimes I forgot that I was in the southern hemisphere and wondered why it got colder as I headed south; I had to remember that September was spring, not fall. Sometimes I had trouble with their accents and slang, and they had trouble with mine.

My intention was not to write a political book. I have never considered myself a "political person." Politics is not a subject in which I have much knowledge or interest. And yet every moment of the weeks I spent in South Africa was totally political. It was inescapable.

I met Whites who despised Blacks and Blacks who hated

Whites and people of all colors who were praying for peace and reconciliation. I met open-minded people and people who seemed to have no idea of what was going on or didn't care. Sometimes I got angry and had to bite my tongue when I encountered arrogance and dislike of America and Americans for our stand against apartheid. Sometimes I made friends with people who took me into their homes and treated me like visiting royalty, people I shall never forget. I have changed their names and disguised their identities, even in some cases the names of their towns. There were several reasons for doing this. Should copies of this book end up in South Africa, it could get some of the more outspoken Blacks and Whites into trouble with a government that can arrest without cause and hold indefinitely without charge. Who knows what might happen to Samuel if his real name were to appear in print as one of the boycott leaders? A paranoid overreaction, perhaps, but fear is endemic in South Africa.

In other cases I simply did not want to embarrass people who were kind to me and who trusted me, believing that I understood and was sympathetic to their point of view. I have been honest in this book in ways that I could not be honest when I was staying in their homes, accepting their hospitality. I liked them, some more than others, but often I thought they were wrong. When they read what I have written about them and about their country, they will recognize themselves. They may feel that I have betrayed them, and in some ways I have. At least I do not have to embarrass them in their communities.

Always I kept notes, trying to get everything down, knowing I was finding much of what I needed but uncomfortably aware that I was missing a lot. There was not enough time to do it all, see it all, ask all the questions I needed to ask and listen to the answers. And there was not always the balance I wanted. As a White among Whites I was on equal ground. There was the luxury of time and ease of communication. As a White among Blacks, things were much more difficult. I had the advantage of being an American and therefore viewed as sympathetic, but White nevertheless with all the wealth, power, and privilege that implies. I could stay in White homes, where conversations ranged on for days. Legally I could not stay in a Black home. Since contacts with Blacks were usually arranged and engineered by Whites, time with Blacks was always short (if I got more than half an hour I was lucky), the situation somewhat contrived, and other people usually present to stifle whatever candid exchanges might have been generated. It was a frustrating situation.

I am not an expert on South Africa. Obviously five weeks in any country does not work that miracle. I am, however, an expert on my own experiences and my own observations during that time. I have attempted to weave my background reading on the subject with what I saw, what I heard, and how I felt, in order to offer you, the reader, a tapestry of what it's like to grow up in this troubled land.

January 15, 1986
ALBUQUERQUE, NEW MEXICO

I

CAPE TOWN

▲ ▲ ▲ ▲ ▲ **C**innamon, pepper, nutmeg, clove—the history of South Africa began with the quest for spices. Since ancient times spices from the Far East had been in great demand in Europe, partly to enliven an otherwise dull diet but mainly as a way to preserve unrefrigerated food or to cover the off-taste of food going bad. Caravans carried spices across China and India to Mediterranean ports, from which they were taken by ship to the cities of Europe and sold at huge profits. When the Mongols and Turks cut off the overland routes, spice-hungry Europeans looked for a different way to move the precious cargo from East to West.

An innovative Italian navigator named Christopher Columbus believed he could reach the East by sailing west. For years he tried doggedly to interest Portugal in backing his plan, but the monarchs of that country had something else in mind. Early in the fifteenth century Portuguese Prince Henry the Navigator had begun sending ships down along the west coast of Africa in search of a sea route to India. But it was not until 1488 that Bartholomew Diaz made it as far as the promontory later called the Cape of Good Hope, and on to the southern tip of the continent, an area of such violent weather that the courageous mariner named it Cabo Tormentoso, or the Sea of Storms. It is likely that on board Diaz's ship was a master chart maker named Bartholomew Columbus, whose brother was still knocking on royal doors in Europe, trying to sell someone on his "Enterprise of the Indies."

In 1497 another Portuguese navigator, Vasco da Gama, pushed farther along Diaz's route, rounding the tip known as Cape Agulhas, a Portuguese word for "needles," referring to its saw-edged reefs. Cape Agulhas is the southernmost point of land, where Atlantic and Indian oceans meet. Gama continued up the east coast of Africa, and on December 25 of that year he sailed into a harbor that he named Port Natal ("Natal" means Christmas), later renamed Durban. By cutting across the Indian Ocean, Gama arrived in India in 1499. His voyage provided Portugal with a sea route to the wealth of the Indies.

For a hundred years the Portuguese kept the riches of the spice trade all to themselves. They paid little attention to that halfway point between home and India, the Cape of Good Hope, where they sometimes put ashore to fill their barrels with fresh water or to barter with the native brown-skinned people for sheep and cattle, or Cape Agulhas, where too often they were washed ashore when Cabo Tormentoso smashed their ships. And no one ever ventured inland.

The high price of spices soon had the European traders at each other's throats over control of the East Indies and the sea routes to reach them. By 1600 the English, Dutch, and French were coming up as strong rivals. A group of powerful businessmen in Holland formed the Dutch East India Company to expand their country's trade with the East. Half a century later the company dispatched a sea captain named Jan van Riebeeck (REE-bake) to the Cape of Good Hope to establish a "refreshment station"—a hospital to care for sick sailors, a fort to protect them when they came ashore, and a source of meat and fresh vegetables. On April 6, 1652, van Riebeeck sailed into Table Bay at the foot of flat-topped Table Mountain with about a hundred men and, by some accounts, a few women on board. The history of what was to become South Africa had begun.

South Africa feels like a big country, and indeed it is: 472,000 square miles, one-eighth the size of the United States, or, put another way, three times the size of California. Located at the southern end of the vast continent of Africa—the second largest continent in the world, of which South Africa represents only 4 percent—it looks like a remote outpost on the map of the world. Cape Town, the former refreshment station, is as far from London on a direct line as Pt. Barrow, Alaska, is from Miami, and for centuries it lay out of the mainstream of developing civilization, floating beyond the eddies and swirls of world history.

Most of the country lies south of the Tropic of Capricorn, which places it in a subtropical latitude. Johannesburg, the largest city, is situated about the same number of degrees south of the equator as southern Texas and Florida are north of the equator. Cape Town's latitude is roughly similar to that of Albuquerque and Memphis. July gets cold and blustery, but many South Africans head for beaches on the Atlantic and Indian oceans over Christmas and New Year's.

Most of the country is high and dry, and rainfall is unpredictable. Farmers search the sky for signs of rain at critical times and hover around the television for the nightly weather

14

report. The Karoo, a name derived from an aboriginal word meaning "place of the great dryness," occupies about a third of South Africa's land surface, and it is steadily spreading into the grasslands. One thing that thrives in the Karoo is sheep—and there are plenty of those. Even along the coast droughts are a fact of life. Only 12 percent of South Africa is fit for cultivation, although in some places the soil is incredibly rich and productive.

Throughout the world rivers have played an important role in the development of most countries, but not in South Africa. Rugged mountains produce spectacular waterfalls, but there is not one navigable river. There are immense mineral resources, but the early settlers had no idea of these treasures hidden beneath the surface. They were simply trying to find a way to survive in a harsh, beautiful land.

Harsh and beautiful, but by no means empty. Nearly ten thousand years before the first Whites came ashore, the area was roamed by the San, people of small stature with light brown skin. Called Bushmen by Whites, the San were nomadic hunters and gatherers of wild food, who shot game with poisoned arrows and toted precious water in ostrich eggshells. They made their mark as artists, leaving behind beautiful rock paintings wherever they lived. For a while the San resisted the intrusion of the Whites, but eventually they stopped resisting and faded away into the stark desert.

The first aboriginal tribes to meet the new settlers around Table Bay were the Khoikhoi, another brown-skinned group related to the San. (Both groups speak a complicated language made up of clicking sounds.) Pastoral people whose enormous herds of sheep and cattle counted as their wealth, the Khoikhoi (dubbed Hottentots by the Dutch) were asked to trade their sheep and cattle for iron, copper, and other desirable items. But the Khoikhoi were unreliable traders. Jan van Riebeeck decided to establish farms and began to bring in more settlers, this time soldiers released from service (known as "free burghers"), to be the farmers.

This turned out to be harder than it first appeared, for the land beyond Table Mountain was not well suited to grazing; it took more land here to support a few head of cattle than on the rich pastures of Europe. The settlers moved inland, and the squeeze for land was already on. Within a few years the Khoikhoi and the San, known collectively as the Khoisan, were driven off their land, killed, or forced into slavery. Most of those who survived were wiped out by smallpox epidemics in the early eighteenth century.

More colonists continued to make the long, hard journey from Holland, joined at the end of the seventeenth century by French Huguenots. The Huguenots were Protestants who followed the teachings of John Calvin, a French theologian. For years they had been persecuted for their beliefs by the Roman Catholic church, but in 1598 the Edict of Nantes, issued by the king of France, granted them freedom of worship and political independence. Their freedom lasted less than a century. Threatened by the number of skilled craftsmen and members of the middle class who were becoming Huguenots, the Catholic-controlled French government began to strip away their rights and in 1685 revoked the Edict of Nantes. The persecuted Huguenots fled to America as well as to other countries of Europe, such as Holland. A few years later Simon van der Stel, who had been appointed governor of the colony established on the Cape of Good Hope, persuaded a few hundred Huguenot refugees in Holland to try their luck in this new country. The French brought to the Cape their particular skills, especially in agriculture and viticulture—growing grapes for wine. Soon vineyards were thriving in the fertile valleys around Cape Town, and French names became as common as Dutch in the colony.

Then the Dutch East India Company hired four thousand

German peasants to establish farms in the Cape Colony. It was the intermarriage of Dutch, German, and French that produced the White South Africans known as Afrikaners, a group that had established a strong identity through culture and language—Afrikaans, a derivative of Dutch—by the time the first British arrived in the Cape in 1795. It was Simon van der Stel's son, Willem, the next governor of the Cape Colony in the early 1700s, who sneeringly referred to the Afrikaners as *boers*, the Dutch word for farmers. Willem did not last long as governor, but the name stuck.

Since the Khoisan had all along stubbornly refused to work for the White men, the farmers solved their labor problems by importing Black slaves, from West and East Africa and from the islands of the East Indies, such as Java. As inevitably as Dutch, German, and French intermingled, so did White Europeans with non-Whites. Mixed-blood descendants of wifeless White settlers and the Khoisan, the Javanese (themselves mixes of Chinese, Indians, and other groups) and the Black Africans are designated by the South African government as "Coloureds," one of the four official racial categories. The Coloured label is shunned by many mixed-race people, who term it "so-called Coloureds," or write it within quotation marks, or say it with the two-fingered gestures of both hands that signify quotation marks. The government has broken the Coloured classification down even further: Griquas, descended from the Khoisan, Cape Malays from the Javanese, and a category called Others.

Cape Town is a knuckle on a finger that beckons into the sea, a peninsula jutting into the Atlantic Ocean. You couldn't ask for a prettier city. You can stroll through cobbled streets lined with quaint buildings, picturesque squares, and flower markets. You can take a cable car up Table Mountain and enjoy a spectacular view of the city and the meeting of great oceans. You can ride a train through luxurious suburbs with plummy-sounding English names—Rosebank, Claremont, Kenilworth, Newlands—past well-groomed tennis courts lively with people in tennis whites, gracious homes with perfectly manicured lawns, shopping centers with attractive stores and places to relax with an afternoon cup of tea.

The early White settlers in the Cape were homesick, of course, and they often built houses that reminded them of home. But they were also practical people, adapting their memories to the climate and to the materials available—thick walls with ornate, curlicued gables, a string of rooms fronting on a long porch called a stoep (pronounced STOOHP), the whole thing whitewashed to a gleam and topped with a roof of thatch like neatly barbered hair. The interiors were finished in rich, dark stinkwood and bright yellowwood, and the same contrasting woods were used to fashion handsome furniture with simple lines. Known as "Cape Dutch" style, it is a unique contribution to the world of architecture and one of the most striking aspects of Cape Town.

Rosebank and Newlands were not the names appearing in the news. Headlines pinpointed Langa, Athlone, Mitchell's Plain, called "townships" or "locations," places where the non-Whites live, Coloureds descended from the long-dead builders of the gleaming white farmhouses, Blacks and Asians who have come to the Cape peninsula from other parts of South Africa looking for work.

Most Coloureds live in the western part of the Cape Province, and most of them live on the peninsula. Once there was an area in the middle of Cape Town known as District Six. To some it was the vital, throbbing heart of the Coloured community, to others a disgusting slum. To the government District Six was a "black spot" in the midst of a White area, and for that reason it had to be erased. A dozen years ago the residents were driven out and bulldozers razed their homes, reducing District Six to twelve acres of rubble.

With no place to go, those who had been removed gathered in squatters' settlements at a dusty, windy place outside of Cape Town known as Crossroads—more than thirty thousand people huddled in tar-paper shacks. Government attempts to obliterate it failed, and Crossroads slowly developed into a well-established community. But it too became overcrowded—there were eventually a hundred thousand Coloureds in the area—and spawned another squatter camp, New Crossroads. Now the government has created a township called Khayelitsha and is forcibly removing people from New Crossroads to the new township, miles further from Cape Town, where they work.

Mary McChesney

Mary McChesney, a lawyer's wife, lives in one of those charming Cape Dutch houses furnished with antiques. The house looks rich, but Mary dresses austerely in a serviceable suit without jewelry, and her car verges on rattletrap. Mary has servants, of course—most Whites do—but she is as liberal a woman as one is likely to find in the Cape. Although most women of her social class do not have jobs or careers, Mary prefers to spend her time teaching in Coloured schools. Her subject is history, and it's a frustrating undertaking. "Futile," she said. "The students simply don't have the facility to express themselves in English, the language we're required to use. And the African languages aren't suited to instruction in sciences."

There is not much for her to do now, though, with the boycotts in effect, and so she offered to drive me around to places she thought I would find interesting. A visiting American, she confessed, was like an exotic pet to show off.

"I know how it must look to you," she said, "the White

19

lawyer's wife, living in a beautiful house with servants and running around being liberal and outspoken—and safe. I also know what would happen if some of the things I'm working for came to pass. I'd lose all this." She waved at the house and well-groomed lawn centered with a jewel of a swimming pool.

It was Mary who introduced me to Samuel Mkunqwana at St. Jerome's. And now, just before noon, she proposed to take me to Belgravia High School in the township of Athlone. "Very middle-class Coloured," she said.

The brick buildings were surrounded by a chain link fence, the gates closed but not locked. A student on a bicycle opened a gate for us. It seemed peaceful to me, but Mary pointed out that the streets were lined with parked cars, several people sitting quietly in each. "Parents," she explained. "Something must be going on."

Incongruously, three horses grazed on the school lawn as we entered the building, past signs set up for a first-aid station. Inside the principal's office half a dozen Coloured teachers clustered by the window, turning to stare at us as we came in. They looked terrified, frozen in mid-gesture like animals trapped in a spotlight. No one moved; no one spoke. Mary sized up the situation, apologized to the teachers, and pulled me outside. "They're expecting trouble," she said.

Students drifted toward the building. The parents stood outside their cars now, hovering anxiously but doing nothing. Down the street a Casspir, one of the ominous-looking armored police vehicles, maneuvered into position. From the opposite direction a troop of students, teenage boys, marched silently across an empty field from a nearby high school toward Belgravia.

"Now comes a bloody confrontation," Mary predicted. "Do you want to stay around and watch?" Like many others, Mary believes the police stimulate violence in order to put it down, flexing their muscles and showing the rioters who is in charge.

I rejected her invitation. I could read about it in the morning paper. As we drove off, one of the horses was rolling playfully in the grass.

Cape Times, Thursday, September 5, 1985:

> RUNNING BATTLES IN ATHLONE RIOT. Running street battles between police and students erupted in Belgravia, Athlone, yesterday afternoon as youths erected at least 30 burning barricades and flung rocks and petrol bombs at police vehicles. . . .
>
> The violence erupted at 1.45 pm during a mass rally at Belgravia High School attended by at least 4 000 pupils and students from 24 high schools. . . . After a ceremonial burying of a coffin labelled "Apartheid", students massed in the school quad. Six police vans, a Casspir and a video unit watched as students sang freedom songs. . . . As speakers appealed to the crowd not to provoke the police because 'that will give them an excuse', a group of about 200 youths lit a barricade. . . . A Casspir moved in, firing teargas canisters and rubber bullets into the school grounds as the crowd fled.

Myrtle's Family

Mary whisked me away from impending disaster in Athlone and dropped me off in Mitchell's Plain, another area of unrest, for a quick visit with Myrtle, her maid. Myrtle has been "in service" with Mary for eighteen years, and she had invited me through Mary to meet her stepson, Donald. On

21

the way, Mary filled me in on family history. After being shunted about for years, Donald has recently come to live with his father, Myrtle's new husband.

Their home was one of many small, tidy houses with fake Greek pillars ornamenting the front porch, where Donald and his friend Linda were waiting. They took me inside to sit at the polished dining table in the main room, decorated with crocheted doilies and plastic flowers. An oil painting in bright primary colors hung in the place of honor high above the sofa. I found the signature: *M. McChesney.* A dog in the backyard leaped on his hind legs and yapped insistently at the window.

Donald, seventeen, has a long thin face, slightly Oriental eyes, and a wispy moustache. He is either quite withdrawn, or uncomfortable speaking English, or ill at ease with the White American writer who has come to ask him questions. Maybe all three. Although he had dressed up in a blue sport shirt for my visit he was obviously relieved to let the conversation focus on Linda, a fifteen-year-old who was all shy smiles and sweet charm. Her curly hair was braided in a single thick plait.

As a condition of the visit I had promised not to bring up politics, a subject that frightens most parents as much as it stimulates most of their children. Myrtle sat there with us, her hands folded in her lap, and I could not say to them, "Tell me what you think, what you *feel.*" And I couldn't ask what they thought of the boycott.

Instead I asked Linda about her family. Her mother, she said, works for a very rich lady who travels—"Everywhere, even to America"—and employs Linda's mother to knit clothes exclusively for her. (Mary said later she had never heard of such a thing, a personal knitter.) Linda's stepfather has been living with them for several years. "Do you get along with him?" I asked.

She shrugged. "I just don't pay him any attention."

We talked about how nice it would be to have a car, lots of money. There seemed to be no way to get beneath the surface, not with Myrtle there.

When Myrtle's niece Grace came in and joined us, the lagging conversation caught some of her energy. A vivacious woman in her twenties, she had been laid off from her job in a dress shop where she did secretarial work.

"What will you do now?"

"Look for a job. Every Monday and Wednesday jobs are listed in the paper, but there are many applicants. Many people are unemployed here."

"There is supposed to be unemployment compensation," Myrtle said, "but some have signed up for it week after week for months on end and never collect any money."

I asked if she would consider going into service as a domestic, like her mother and her aunt. Domestic service is still the main source of employment for Coloured women in Cape Town. "I'm depressed, but not *that* depressed," she said with a wry laugh.

"Maybe you should find a rich husband," I suggested, hoping she would understand that I was joking.

"That's the same as being in service," she shot back. Myrtle smiled.

The boycott was never mentioned. Neither was the violence in the schoolyard only a few miles away. They were polite, entertaining a foreign visitor. When Mary picked me up half an hour later, I knew no more than I had in the first place.

Ahmed Kumar

Mr. Kumar called late one evening after I had fallen asleep, but his conversation had me awake in an instant. He would agree to see me under one condition: that I promise I was not an agent for the CIA. It was the first time anyone ever suggested that I might be a spy, and I had to admit that posing as an author of books for young adults might be the perfect cover for someone in the espionage business. I was also fascinated that he assumed I would tell him the truth, if I *were* a spy.

The next afternoon his brother escorted me into the lounge, as South Africans call a living room. Mr. Kumar was finishing his lunch; silverware clinked behind the closed door to the kitchen. There was an expensive stereo system, a plush-covered sectional sofa with crocheted doilies along the backs and arms, framed illustrations on the walls decorated with Indian script. The scent of incense floated lightly in the air.

Mr. Kumar carried in a tea tray, poured me a cup, and told me his story. A teacher in an Indian high school, he is in his mid-twenties, darkly handsome with a radiant smile that gleams through a thick black beard. His father is a successful businessman and a Muslim leader, and the large Kumar clan lives in a two-family brick house that has been remodeled into one big home with plenty of room for the various Kumar brothers and sisters. I admired his house, and he nodded his thanks.

"The problem now is how long we can keep it. This house has belonged to our family for many years, but it is in a White area. The government will force us to move."

Ahmed Kumar is part of the small Indian population of the Cape; most Indians live in the province of Natal, where the first immigrants came in 1860 to work on the sugar plantations. The government classifies them as part of the official racial group known as Asians. The attractive street on which the Kumars live used to be part of the Indian community, but the charming old houses, gabled and thatched, are now considered very chic by the Whites in this suburb. All of the other Indian families have been removed by the government, just as the Coloured families were taken away from District Six, but the Kumars somehow have managed to hold onto their home.

"Every few weeks government officials come banging on the door to harass us, urging us but not yet forcing us to get out. Since no comparable housing has been found for us in an Asian area, we are safe for a while longer."

The government's definition of "comparable" does not necessarily mean of equal size or value, he says, but no one knows quite what it does mean. "I believe that God is protecting us," Ahmed said. "It would be dangerous for us to live in an area where the Indians elected to the farcical legislature live. A few of them may be working for change, but most of them are hated as collaborators. Their homes are being petrol bombed. Who would want to be their neighbors?"

Ahmed has a theory about why his culture is so much healthier, his people so much better off than the Coloureds. "We are Muslim," he said, "and Muslims are prohibited by their faith from being involved with a government that practices apartheid. But even more important, Muslims do not drink alcohol."

Everyone acknowledges that alcoholism is the major problem among Coloureds. Wine growers used to pay their Coloured workers partly "in kind," sometimes as much as three bottles a day, to keep them docile if not downright drunk. Later that was cut down to a *dop*—a bottle or two—at the end of the week, but the pattern was strongly established: people drank because they were given wine, drank because it deadened the pain of their lives. The pattern was perpetuated: babies were born to alcoholic parents who gave them wine to quiet them, just as their *baas* (boss; master) gave *them* wine to quiet them.

When our tea was finished, Mr. Kumar walked with me

to the railway station, past pretty houses and attractive shops. On the way I asked him why he thought I might be a CIA agent. He smiled his dazzling smile. "The principal of my school insisted that I ask you. With so much bad happening, he is suspicious of everybody. Everyone is afraid of everyone else."

I waited for the train back to the center of Cape Town, remembering to stand at the section of the platform where cars marked "Whites Only/Nie Blankie" would stop, ensuring that I would not sit with Coloureds. They rode in separate cars at the end of the train.

II

STELLENBOSCH

▲ ▲ ▲ ▲ ▲ **T**he road winds past lush vineyards and picture-book farms. Handsome Cape Dutch buildings cluster around the Braak, the town square of Stellenbosch, founded in 1679 by Simon van der Stel. Not far from the Braak is the University of Stellenbosch, one of ten residential universities for Whites in South Africa. Five conduct lectures in the Afrikaans language, four in English, and one is "dual medium," using both. Stellenbosch teaches in Afrikaans. It is the academic center of Afrikanerdom, the culture that evolved from the melding of Dutch, German, and French.

Spoken by close to three million people, Afrikaans developed slowly during two centuries of settlement, evolving from the Dutch spoken by the Boers around the middle of the nineteenth century. Most of the vocabulary derived from Dutch, but new words were added and others adopted from other languages: German and French, which were part of the ethnic mixture, as well as Malay, Portuguese, Khoisan, English, and African tongues. The pronunciation of Afrikaans is much different from Dutch. It is quite guttural; some English speakers claim it sounds like someone with a bad cough. For instance, *g* in Afrikaans sounds like a German *ch*. *V* is pronounced like *f*; *w* sounds like *v*; *a* has a long sound, as in "wand." The name van Wyck, for example, would be pronounced "fahn VAKE." The grammar of Dutch has been greatly simplified, the old rules thrown out. As a result, Hollanders cannot understand Afrikaans and scorn it as an unintelligible "kitchen dialect." Linguists say there are similarities between Afrikaans and the Flemish language spoken in Belgium; Flemish has much in common with the Dutch language as it was spoken centuries ago.

Regardless of what language it resembles, Afrikaans did not exist as a written language until about 1870. The Boers were not readers; the Bible was their only book, and that was written in Dutch, the formal language of their religion. After the arrival of English people and the change of rule from Dutch to British in the early 1800s, English became the language of government, except in the northern areas where Dutch remained official. But Afrikaans was really at the heart of the development of "Afrikanerdom," the sense the Afrikaners had of being a unique community. Afrikaans began to gain wider acceptance after it became a written language, but not until 1925 was it recognized as the second official language of South Africa, in addition to English and replacing Dutch.

The year after this recognition scholars at Stellenbosch set to work compiling an Afrikaans dictionary. By 1978 they had progressed as far as letter *K* (there is no *C* in Afrikaans) and published six volumes. Not far from Stellenbosch, overlooking the Paarl Valley, enthusiasts erected the Afrikaans Language Monument dedicated to the early champions of the new language. The various curves and forms supposedly represent Western, Eastern, and African influences on Afrikaans.

Religion was as important as language to Afrikanerdom. South Africa has no state church, but the Dutch Reformed church (in Afrikaans, Nederduitse Gereformeerd Kerk) has been there the longest, claims the most members (about 90 percent of all Afrikaners belong to the NGK), and exercises the most influence. The Reformed church emerged in Holland in the sixteenth century, founded on the teachings of John Calvin, whose followers had included the French Huguenots. Calvinists believe that God's will is absolute; they also believe that God chooses to save some people and not to save others, and that there is nothing a person can do to earn salvation or to change God's will.

The first member of the Dutch Reformed church to arrive in South Africa was Jan van Riebeeck himself. He went ashore, took one look at the naked, brown-skinned people staring back at him, and prayed to God to make him and his men the means for bringing the Reformed faith to the heathens of Africa.

But the directors of the Dutch East India Company were no more interested in organizing missionary work than they were in colonizing southern Africa. Meanwhile, men called "comforters of the sick" did what they could to take care of the spiritual problems of the early White settlers. They waited for a *predikant*, or minister, who might be passing by on one of the company's ships to stop off and give them Communion. In 1665 a *predikant* came ashore to stay and established the first Dutch Reformed congregation. As the Boers pushed inland, they formed new congregations wherever they settled. All these new churches needed *predikants* to lead them, and in 1859 a theological seminary was founded at Stellenbosch to train them.

As for van Riebeeck's plans for Christianizing the heathen,

many of the Khoisan and the Black slaves were converted, baptized, and then freed. But the early churchmen waffled on whether brown- and black-skinned people should actually worship with the White settlers. On the one hand, the leaders argued piously, it was both "desirable and scriptural" that Khoisan and Blacks be "received and absorbed into our existing congregations wherever possible." But they realized that not all the Whites would accept such a notion. If, because of the "weakness" (in other words, racial prejudice) of some of their brethren, having a mixed congregation should somehow get in the way of the main job of converting the heathen, then those heathen would have to "enjoy their Christian privileges in a separate building or institution."

Quite a few Whites did apparently suffer from the kind of weakness that required the new converts to worship someplace else. Eventually the whole (White) church came to the conclusion that the Gospel had to be preached to non-Whites in a different way, tailored to their capacity to absorb it. Most Whites then, like many Whites now, viewed non-Whites as intellectually inferior. The poor quality of non-White education has reinforced that belief. That meant establishing separate congregations, a separation that still exists. The NGK is divided into three sections, each for a specific racial group. The World Alliance of Reformed Churches suspended the Dutch Reformed church for its "heresy" of racial segregation in 1982. Allan Boesak, head of the Coloured section, was elected Alliance president. The NGK is no longer a member of the World Council of Churches or the South African Council of Churches.

It is ironic that most of the 2.6 million people classified as Coloured belong to the Dutch Reformed church. (Anglican, Roman Catholic, and Methodist churches all oppose apartheid.) The Coloureds share with the Afrikaners not only their religion but also their language and much of their culture. They have often been called "brown Afrikaners."

François and Marianne du Plessis

A framed, illuminated chart on the wall of the lounge traces the du Plessis line through eight generations, all the way back to seventeenth-century France. That first du Plessis —also named François—arrived with his wife with the first group of Huguenot settlers in 1688. The son of that couple married a Potgieter, their son married a Steyn, the next a Malan, and so on through a Meyer, a Visser, then a van Wyck. Marianne's name has not been added to the chart, though, because her maiden name was Taylor. No one in François's family has ever married a woman with an English background. His family did not speak to him for years, until his daughters were teenagers.

Her family, the Taylors, were not much more cordial. Usually, in mixed-marriage situations, the husband follows the wife, but not in this case. Marianne left the Anglican church to join the Dutch Reformed church with her husband. Furthermore, she learned to speak Afrikaans, and that is what they speak at home.

Marianne and François met at the University of Stellenbosch when they were students. It is somewhat unusual for a girl of English background to attend Stellenbosch; most of the twelve thousand students are Afrikaners. When François decided to stay on and complete a doctorate, Marianne made an earnest effort to learn Afrikaans. She speaks precisely, but with an English accent. Most of their friends are Afrikaners, and François is now on the faculty. Marianne has always run her household in Afrikaans. The children are bilingual, but they usually speak Afrikaans, too.

We sat in the lounge, having walked the four family dogs in the hills above the vineyards after François came home from his office, and he had uncorked a bottle of local red wine. Two of the dogs, a shepherd and a Lab, stalked up and down outside the French doors, staring in. Two rat-sized chihuahuas lorded it over the outdoor dogs from their places on the laps of François and Marianne. One of the girls, Suzanne, attends boarding school in Cape Town, and her parents were anxious to get her home for the weekend, before the restlessness and violence got worse and Suzie found herself in trouble.

"Hooligans," snorted Marianne du Plessis. "Those youngsters are just making trouble for the thrill of it." Unlike Mary McChesney, she had little understanding and less sympathy for angry Blacks and Coloureds who were "making trouble" by setting up barricades along the main highway from Cape Town past the airport. Many of them were the same boys and young men boycotting the schools. There is a hooligan element in the violence, the degree depending on one's viewpoint: liberals contending that it is quite small, and conservatives like Marianne arguing just the opposite.

Stellenbosch is considered a stronghold of what some call *verligte* Afrikanerdom, those people who believe the apartheid system should be changed to make it more humane but who are not so liberal that they would agree to share power with the other racial groups; reform apartheid, but don't abolish it. François du Plessis is *verligte*, and so—despite her views of the "hooligans"—is Marianne. Opposed to the *verligte* (which means "enlightened ones") are the *verkrampten*, narrow-minded people set like cement against any kind of change. A large number of top government officials, including State President P. W. Botha, are Stellenbosch alumni; Botha himself is often described as *verligte*.

Opinion as to who is "behind" the riots varies considerably. Some blame it on the Communists, and there may be some accuracy to that. Some, like Marianne, blame it on hooligans, young thugs more interested in destruction and looting than in "the struggle." And some even recognize that the Blacks have legitimate grievances and are resorting to

32

what they feel is the only means available to make themselves heard.

The next day Marianne took me on a tour of the university. It did not look much different from American universities, except for the underground library. A founding father had donated a piece of land in the middle of the campus with the understanding that it be used only as a park. But the university badly needed a new library; the park was the obvious place to build it. And so a huge cave was hollowed out beneath the founding father's lawn and shrubbery and a bright, modern library installed. A good idea, but Marianne said there had been problems: the soil in the park killed all the flowers and shrubs and had to be carted off and re-placed, an embarrassment at a university where agriculture is a major department. Flights of brick steps lead down to the entrance, forming an amphitheater, a natural place to set up some amps, plug in a couple of guitars, and entertain students lounging on the steps in the sunshine over lunch break.

Styles in Stellenbosch that spring were big shirts, long skirts, hip-riding belts, baggy pants, pointy shoes in shiny leather, glaring colors, spiky hair in peculiar shades, and slightly outrageous makeup. Marianne shuddered at the combinations worn by the students; she sews her own ele-gant clothes in silk and linen and makes most of her daugh-ters' outfits, too.

We passed a group of students who were speaking Eng-lish. "I thought this was an Afrikaans university," I said.

"The English are snobbish," she said. "I should know; I'm one of them. They won't bother to speak Afrikaans unless they have to, and if there's one English speaker in the group the nine Afrikaners will switch to accommodate him. But the English still call the Afrikaners all kinds of derogatory names,

like 'rocks' and 'hairy backs.' The English think the Afrikaners are stupid," she said. "They're wrong."

St. Gus

The waves of anger that shook the townships around Cape
Town could not be felt in Stellenbosch, thirty miles from the
epicenter. There was no problem visiting a primary school
here. St. Augustine's is a Roman Catholic school, partly supported by the government. There was no boycott. School
was in session. But there was another problem: it was exam
time.

Nevertheless, Sister Madeline offered to help. "Let me see
what I can salvage for you," she said and disappeared into
another building. In a few minutes she was back, followed
by a dozen uniformed children, girls in navy blue jumpers
and starched white blouses, boys in navy blue shorts, white
shirts, and neckties. They lined up in front of me and cho-
rused, "Good morning, Madam. We hope you are well. God
bless you, Madam."

This was my first introduction to two of the many differences between U.S. and South African schools: uniforms and
classroom discipline. Uniforms are standard in all schools,
government or private, rich or poor. Whole classes immediately rise when a teacher or other adult enters the room,
make some sort of greeting in unison, and usually rise again
when the adult leaves. It comes as a surprise if you're not
used to it.

This group of Coloured children were Standard Fives, in
their last year at St. Gus, ready to move on to high school
next term. They had just finished their exam in English, their
second language. Sister Madeline found a room for us, joined
by the school mascot, a furry dog named Buffy. Buffy was

a great handshaker, and his pawing gave me something to do while I tried to figure out what to say to a dozen giggling twelve-year-olds, four boys being only slightly rambunctious on one side of the room, eight girls perched primly on the other.

I found a way to amuse them: I tried to pronounce their names and write them in a notebook. It was partly the accent; when I couldn't catch a name, and I generally could not, I asked them to spell it, and somehow even that escaped me. How could letters of the alphabet sound so differently when pronounced in a different accent? I sometimes didn't even recognize my own surname, Meyer, when I heard it. (They pronounced it MAY-er, with a rolled *r*; I say it MY-er.) And because Meyer is a common name among Afrikaners (stemming from the same German ancestors, I suppose), they assumed that I would manage better than I did.

There was no such thing as talking out of turn, let alone discussion, in that group. If I proposed a topic ("Tell me about your families") their responses always came counterclockwise, since that was how we began with the naming. Then I asked them what they wanted to do when they had finished school.

Their backgrounds were solid working class, their parents carpenters, machinists, leather workers, a nurse, a printer, a few teachers. But these were not the lives to which they aspired. Michelle, a tall girl with glasses and braids, was the first to answer all the questions because she sat on the end of the sofa. She said she wanted to be a doctor. Michelle's answer may have prompted three of the boys to say they wanted to be doctors, one a lawyer. The girls were divided between doctor, artist, ballet dancer (the girl had never seen a ballet), teacher. I remembered the poster on the principal's wall in another school. They were certainly dreaming big.

Before I left, Michelle ran off to find me a copy of the St.

Gus school magazine, filled with poetry in Afrikaans and news stories in English about new soccer jerseys and pink-and-white costumes for the drum majorettes, "Looking a bit like those big ice-creams advertised outside the shops in town, and as beautiful as we looked, so beautifully did we step it out to the tune of 'Colonel Bogey'." One of the major items had to do with their latest dramatic production, *Snow White*. Did anyone but me find that an ironic choice when all the actors were Coloured, or was the irony intentional? St. Gus didn't seem like the kind of place where tongue-in-cheek would thrive.

Sister Madeline was not interested in talking about soccer jerseys and majorette costumes. She was worried about the boycott.

"I've explained it to the pupils. I tell them to read news-papers and watch television. There is great sympathy for the boycott, especially among the teachers, but the parents are ambivalent. They struggled hard for what they have. They helped each other to learn trades and work their way up. They want their children to have what they did not: a good education, a good job, a good life. Yet they understand that sacrifices have to be made—maybe a year of schooling. Maybe much more than that."

As always, the nun said, it was the students who were caught in the middle, squeezed by teachers on one side, the parents on the other. "The teachers are very restless. They back the boycott. They want to be with their students, but the students do not always feel that solidarity." The students, for their own reasons, had voted by a narrow margin to postpone the boycott, at least until they were through with their exams.

On their way to lunch the Standard Fives saw me leave Sister Madeline's office. "Good-bye, Madam!" they cho-rused. "Be well! God bless you!"

Clinton Willemse

In a valley near Stellenbosch, a green place between rugged mountains with a noisy stream close by and fields of trellised grapevines pruned back to the main branches, Clinton Willemse waited at home with nothing to do. His mother, Tillie, has been Marianne's "char" (maid) for years. Every day Tillie walks a couple of miles to town to Marianne's house, and every day Marianne drives her home to the valley after work. At harvesttime Tillie will have to take some days off, because the farmers always require the wives of their laborers to pitch in with the grape picking, at significantly lower wages than are paid to their husbands.

A good-looking woman, Tillie hides her kinky hair under a headcloth. Straight, White-style hair is much desired by some Coloureds. "The goal," Marianne said, "is to be able to wear curlers. That shows a woman is of a higher social order, closer to being White." It is not just her hair that Tillie feels she must hide. According to Marianne she's a very bright woman who "married down," and her farm-laborer husband is far beneath her. She is hard pressed to disguise her brains.

On the way out from town, Marianne told me about her char's family. "Tillie's daughter, Cydaria, aspired to be a beautician. She was going to beauty school when she fell pregnant"—("to fall pregnant" seems to be a peculiarly South African phrase)—"and now Cydaria's two children, Emile and Lucinda, live with Tillie."

"Clinton is his mother's hope. Her first son died, and since that happened she has overprotected Clinton to such an extent that he is now a nervous wreck. I don't know what will become of him."

His watchful mother will not let Clinton be politicized, let alone radicalized, and it is possible that she may be able to shield him from "the struggle." Most parents cannot. Over and over I heard it said that teenagers, fed up with their parents' moderate attitude, have reversed roles, taken over, rejecting the White values that kept their parents in their place. But not in this home. Tillie is still in charge. She had invited Ezra, a neighbor, to join the conversation, explaining to Marianne that this might make it easier for Clinton to talk to me. But, like Myrtle in Cape Town, she hovered.

Tillie's home is an imitation Cape Dutch cottage provided by the owner of the vineyard, one of half a dozen built on the farm within the past few years. Tillie has decorated it with bouquets of plastic flowers and lacy crocheted doilies that stand up in stiff ruffles in the middle of each table. The ground around the house was still muddy from the winter rains (Cape winters are wet), and the air was heavy with the scent of jasmine.

Clinton, eighteen, is in his next-to-last year at Luckhoff High School—or he would be if the school were open. He might like to be a teacher, he said, following the example of Ezra, a first-year student at the University of the Western Cape, for Coloureds. Ezra is the first person from this picturesque valley to attend the university. He is studying for a teaching degree in physical education. (There are four universities for Blacks in South Africa, and one each for Coloureds and Indians. Non-Whites who want full-time programs not available at their own universities can sometimes get into White schools. A correspondence school, Unisa, accepts students of all races.)

I wanted to talk about the boycott, but they didn't, at least not with Tillie there.

"Do you support the boycott?" I asked when Tillie left the room for a few moments.

They shook their heads. "I have been pressured to observe the boycott," Ezra said, "and so I came home. But I am studying on my own."

"I was in Athlone two days ago," I said softly. "At Belgravia High School."

They leaned forward intently. "What was it like? What was happening?" Ezra asked.

"Did you take pictures?" Clinton wanted to know.

Tillie came back. Conversation withered.

As I did at other times when the conversation seemed to be running out of gas, I suggested that they ask *me* questions and shift to safer grounds.

"Have you ever seen Michael Jackson?" they asked.

PART TWO

The Heart of the Country

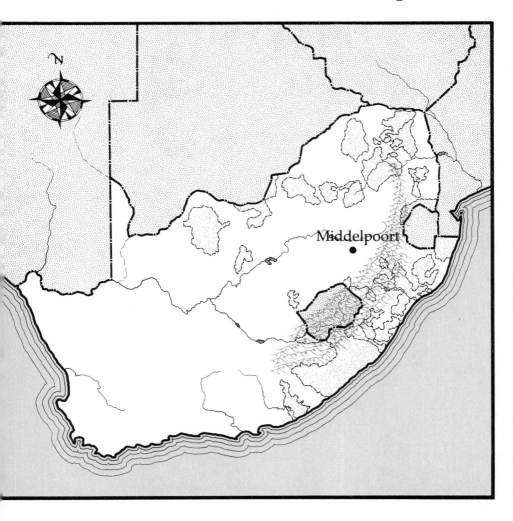

Middelpoort

III

WHITE MIDDELPOORT

▲ ▲ ▲ ▲ ▲   **T**he white Mercedes streaked toward Middelpoort, the name I have given a small farming community that lies just off the N3, the main highway from Johannesburg in the interior to Durban on the east coast. I sat up front next to Koos, an Afrikaner who was hurrying to get home and did not want to struggle with his English while he drove.

Like most highways in South Africa, the two-lane N3 felt narrower than U.S. roads, maybe because I was not yet used to being on the left-hand side, maybe because the shoulders are seldom paved, possibly because the lanes actually *are* narrower. The road was heavily trafficked with lorries (the British word for large trucks) and *bakkies* (the Afrikaans word for pickups), assorted derelict vehicles jammed with Blacks, and pedestrians. We whipped past Blacks walking on the edge of the road, balancing large, awkward-looking loads on their heads. I glanced at the speedometer; the needle hovered at 160 k. The formula for converting kilometers to miles is to divide by eight and multiply by five, and when I figured that in my head I was sorry I had. South Africa's highway fatality rate is among the highest in the world. They say most accidents take place in urban areas—small comfort when you are rocketing down a narrow country road at a hundred miles per hour. Seat belts are mandatory, and South Africans are scrupulous about obeying that law. At least we were all buckled up.

Middelpoort is in the province of the Orange Free State, the heart of the country between the Orange and Vaal rivers. But there are no oranges in the Free State, Koos joked, nothing is free, and the state of things is terrible—usually the weather. Koos owns one of the most prosperous farms in the area, but his prosperity depends at least in part on the rainfall, and drought in the Free State is a fact of life. Maize, called mealies in South Africa and corn in the United States, is the main crop, but the Free State also grows sunflowers, valued for the oil.

It was early spring in the highveld, a treeless grassland. In every direction, as far as the eye could see, the land rolled off in shades of blond and beige, winter grass and the stubble of mealie-lands—cornfields. Flat-topped sandstone ridges called *koppies* dotted the horizon. Hundreds of grazing sheep blended into the beige. When the spring rains came, the landscape would turn lush green. Meanwhile the feed reserves for the cattle had been nearly used up. There was, in late August, only enough to last four more weeks. If the rains did not arrive soon to green up the pastures, Koos would have to buy feed. The air was so still that the windmills stood motionless, and Koos was rushing home to work on a generator that would operate the pump to bring up water for the animals.

Koos (rhymes with "puss") is the fourth generation of his

44

family to live on this farm. His great-grandfather built "Kaalplaats"—Bare Farm—when he arrived as one of the first settlers in the area, a member of the Great Trek.

The Great Trek, as every South African schoolchild learns from the earliest grades, began in 1834. For years before that, *trekboers*, wandering farmers, had been pushing eastward in search of new grazing land. They were also trying to escape the iron hand of the Dutch East India Company, represented by such men as Willem van der Stel, who took over governing the Cape Colony from his father at the beginning of the eighteenth century and had become thoroughly despised.

From the beginning the *trekboers* had simply helped themselves to whatever land they wanted. But in 1770 at the Great Fish River to the east, they first encountered Black people who had been migrating southward from central Africa, also in search of water and grazing land. These wandering Black farmers on the Fish River were the Xhosa (pronounced KOH-suh by English speakers, who have difficulty with the "click" sound of the X).

The confrontation between White and Black cattlemen led to a series of nine battles over the next century known as the Kaffir Wars. (*Kaffir* is an Arabic word meaning "unbeliever." It took on a derogatory sense, similar to the American use of "nigger.") Hemmed in by the Xhosa to the east and by the dry, empty Karoo to the north and northeast, the *trekboers* were halted. Years passed before they eventually reached the other side of the Orange River, the area that became the Orange Free State.

Meanwhile, as a result of political shifts in Europe, an expeditionary force of British soldiers had taken control of the Cape of Good Hope in 1795. In 1803 a treaty returned the Cape to the Dutch, but three years later the British were back. This was a "temporary" arrangement until 1814, when the Cape was placed permanently in British hands.

The British idea of governing a colony was to turn all their subjects into Englishmen, beginning with their language. It was an approach that did not work with the stubborn Afrikaners; in fact, it infuriated them. They decided to put as much distance as they could between themselves and the hated British.

Trek is an Afrikaans word meaning "a slow, arduous journey." In 1834 some four to six thousand men and women—about 10 percent of the White population of the Cape—abandoned their settled lives, loaded a few treasured possessions into lumbering ox wagons, left their homes and began a slow, arduous journey. The Voortrekkers, as these Boers were called, had no idea what they were trekking *toward*; they knew well enough what it was they were leaving, and they risked everything for their vision of freedom—to be clear of the oppressive British. The Great Trek marked a turning point in South African history, and the Voortrekkers became celebrated as the country's folk heroes.

The ox wagons labored in caravans across vast open spaces, camping for long periods and then moving on. For several years the Voortrekkers managed to coexist with groups of Coloureds and Blacks, or at least to fight them off. Attacks on the caravans were frequent, but the Boers knew how to defend themselves: they drew their wagons into a circle and wove thornbushes among the wheels to form an impenetrable barrier. They called the circle a *laager* (LAH-ger); as long as they remained inside the *laager* they were safe against the assegais (ASS-eh-gys)—spears—of the Black attackers. The image of the circled wagons laced with thorns is often used to describe the efforts of embattled Afrikaners of the 1980s who try to protect themselves from criticism of apartheid and pressure from the outside world to change the system; critics call it the *"laager* mentality."

Unable to get together on an overall plan, the Voortrekkers split up into groups that went off in several directions. Those

46

in the highveld had to deal with Mzilikazi, a refugee general of the powerful Zulu nation and his Ndebele tribe. Others managed to get their ox wagons over the rugged Drakensberg Mountains into the area of Natal ruled by another Zulu chief, named Shaka. Shaka ordered his half-brother, Dingane, to deal with these Whites. At first Dingane agreed to let the Voortrekkers settle there, but he changed his mind abruptly and massacred the seventy Whites who arrived at his kraal —village—to sign the treaty. Months later a handful of avenging Boers led by Andries Pretorius threw themselves into battle against Dingane and his army of ten thousand warriors.

It was on December 16, 1838, that Pretorius and his followers made a covenant, a deal with God: if the Almighty would help and protect them and "give the foe unto our hands" in this bloody battle, they would forever remember that day as a Day of Thanksgiving in his honor. When the fighting was over, the Boers counted a few men lost in the process of wiping out three thousand Zulu. They called it the Battle of Blood River. Since that day, Afrikaners have faithfully observed the Day of the Covenant. Their victory was all the proof they needed that they were indeed chosen by God. Natal was theirs for the settling and became the first Boer republic. They named it the Republic of Natalia and established a capital at Pietermaritzburg.

As the Voortrekkers moved deep into the interior, the British, as usual, were right on their heels. British merchants in Natalia were made uneasy by the arrival of the rough Boers and complained to their government in England, and the republic was annexed by Britain four years later. But eventually the British gave up trying to deal with the iron-willed Boers and signed an agreement with their leaders recognizing their independence. The Afrikaners were now told they could form republics in the Transvaal, the area north of the Vaal

River, and in the Orange Free State, the heart of the country, while the British retained two colonies, Natal and the Cape. The score at the end of the Great Trek: Boers, 2—Brits, 2.

Koos and Edna van der Merwe

Jacobus Johannes van der Merwe was born in 1838, the year of the Battle of Blood River and the famous Covenant with God. He spent his early life in the ox wagon and in various temporary homes while his parents searched for a place to put down roots. He was in his teens when the family settled at a spot they named "Kaalplaats" and began to build the stone house with the peaked roof and the long stoep. When his father died, Jacobus, the eldest son, took over the farm and passed it on to *his* eldest son, Cornelis Jacob van der Merwe, who willed it to Jacobus Johan, shortened to Koos, the present owner.

Each time the farm was handed down to the next generation, it was divided among the sons, the farmhouse going to the eldest. Now Koos has two thousand hectares (the metric equivalent of about five thousand acres) on which he grazes a thousand head of cattle and innumerable sheep. The problem is that his two sons both want to farm there, and the land cannot be further subdivided to support two men and their families. Koos and his wife, Edna, are keeping their eyes open for another farm to buy when the time is right, maybe from Edna's nephew, Piet, who has unaccountably fallen in love with racing cars and seems not to give a hoot about farming.

Although the highveld is generally treeless, the original Jacobus Johannes van der Merwe planted willows and eucalyptus around his house, and they have thrived. When one had to be cut down a few years ago, Edna polished the stump and carved into it the names of each generation of van der Merwe to have lived in this house with the years of his birth and death. Koos claims he checks the stump regularly to be sure Edna has not yet carved in his death date.

The stone house is surrounded by luxurious gardens, perhaps more accurately described as a park, patrolled by an enormous dog named Ubaba. The gardens are beautifully tended because there are five young men—Edna calls them *bafans*, meaning "teenagers or adolescents"—to care for them. She also has a household staff to cook, clean, wash, and serve.

The house has been added onto by succeeding generations, but Edna has a penchant for remodeling, knocking out walls and putting them somewhere else. The kitchen is her latest project, equipped with a gas refrigerator and freezer, a brightly enameled coal stove, tile floors, and large work spaces. No electrical gadgets; a generator provides electricity for lights at night. Beyond the kitchen is the formal dining room where breakfast and the main noon meal are served. At the other end of the house, past a couple of formal Victorian parlors and bedrooms filled with family antiques, is the cheerfully informal lounge with a cat curled in each chair. A gas stove takes the chill off the room; it is cold in Middelpoort at this time of year. In the evenings Ubaba flops down in front of the stove and snores loudly.

When the two van der Merwe boys lived at home they occupied a small house adjacent to the main house; the *jonkershuis* or "young man's house" is traditional in Afrikaner families. The *jonkershuis* had been turned over to me for my visit. It was seductively easy to settle into the van der Merwe life-style. At seven-thirty in the morning a maid knocked at my door and carried in a tea tray; at eight o'clock breakfast was served in the dining room. When I went back to my room after breakfast, the bed had been made, my nightgown put away, and my toothbrush, which I had carelessly left lying next to the sink, hung primly in the holder.

Somebody should have warned me about breakfast on the farm. Also lunch, and tea, and supper. The food was wheeled in from the kitchen on a cart by the "cook boy," a Black man in his fifties named Easter who heads the kitchen staff, assisted by four women. There was a platter of *boerewors*, homemade sausages submerged in rich gravy; a dozen fried eggs for the three of us; plates of grilled tomatoes, cheese, buttered toast, and fresh fruit; a bowl of mealie pap—hominy, a coarse kind of grits, that soaks up the gravy at a White farmer's table and is the staple diet of rural Blacks.

It was an awesome spread, but scarcely five hours later we sat down again at the same table, this time to the main meal of the day: roast mutton, potatoes, mealie pap, peas, yams, pumpkin, spinach ("Four vegetables," Edna explained; "we always have four vegetables"), fruit salad, green salad, rolls, and an outrageously rich caramel concoction buried under mounds of whipped cream. The leftover dessert reappeared at teatime.

At seven o'clock Koos and Edna turned on the television in the lounge to watch the news in Afrikaans. They ignored political news—U.S. President Ronald Reagan threatening sanctions of South Africa, State President P. W. Botha denouncing foreign sanctions—and waited for the weather report. We talked and nibbled biltong, flaky chips of sun-dried beef, similar to jerky. They were surprised that I liked it; they say most Americans don't. "Once some people I know sent biltong to friends in the U.S. and got a letter back from the Americans saying they planted it but nothing came up," Koos told me with a straight face. Everyone who offered me biltong told me that story.

Conversation stopped when the weatherman came on, reporting on the entire country. No rain yet for the Free State. Koos shook his head and shut off the TV.

Late in the evening when I had consumed the last of the biltong and concluded that there was to be no more food that day, a maid wheeled in the supper cart. They introduced me to *bobotie*, a South African dish that originated with the Cape Malays, combining ground beef, raisins, and almonds, spiced with curry and served with rice and chutney.

I asked what happened to all the leftovers. "The people in the kitchen eat them," she said. "Except for the vegetables. You can't get Blacks to eat vegetables."

Koos van der Merwe is considered one of the most progressive farmers in the area, practicing "cartwheel grazing" —long, narrow fenced pastures radiating out from a central water supply like spokes of a wheel. Black cowboys ride on English saddles, the stirrups dangling on strings, or on "police saddles," cut higher in front and back but still lacking pommels like the Western saddles used on ranches in the United States. (Horses are not indigenous to Africa; they were brought in from Java for the early settlers.)

About 140 Black workers live at Kaalplaats, many of whose families have been on the land as long as Koos's. Those who work for Edna stay in quarters near the main house; the rest go home to small cottages scattered in extended-family clusters on the *veld* (field; pronounced "felt"). Koos prides himself in treating his workers well. He provides houses for them to live in, land to farm, mealie seeds to plant. He gives them vitamin supplements (which he takes himself, in addition to his three hefty meals a day) and drives them to the doctor when they are ill. "Frankly, it is to my advantage to look after their health," he said. "A sick man does no work."

There are about 60,000 White farmers in South Africa, employing some 4.3 million Blacks, the largest and lowest-paid group of workers. Farmers used to pay their workers in food and housing, like the feudal system of the Middle Ages, but a new law requires them to pay cash. Koos's philosophy is to keep the weekly salary low, making it up to his farmhands with a large bonus at the end of the year. "If they get more cash each week they spend it all at once," he says. "And if they have money in their pockets, they just take off whenever they feel like it and leave me shorthanded. As it is, many of them quit as soon as they collect their year-end bonus. I see them again only after it is gone."

The first of September is the time for negotiating new contracts with the workers. Koos told me the story of Isaac, his manager. "Isaac is a good man," he said. "He has worked for me for years. Last year when it came time to renew his contract, I asked him what he wanted. He asked for a few more rands a month. I offered him a very substantial increase if he would be responsible for getting things fixed when they needed it, ordering supplies, making decisions. But Isaac said no—he didn't want the responsibility. He'd rather have only a few extra rands and be allowed to work as he always has. It just shows you," Koos said, to make sure I understood, "that Blacks do not want to work hard, and they don't want responsibility, even for more money. They have no idea of what it means to better themselves."

Edna said, "We love our Blacks. They are like our children." And now she was half-irritated, half-amused at her *bafans*, the teenage boys who work in her garden. Young people know nothing, she says, not even the simplest things. She has had to teach the boys how to use a screwdriver and pliers. And the girls in the house are just as bad. She has instructed them in the kitchen, showed them how to cook and clean up, taught them to knit and crochet. And now the most arrogant, the cheekiest of the boys, Mashobene, has come with a complaint: *Baas* Koos insists that they be at work at eight o'clock sharp. If they are even five minutes late, he is angry with them. But last evening *Baas* kept them until ten minutes after their five o'clock quitting time to help unload the licks for the cattle. It is unfair for him to insist that they come on time and then keep them late.

I watched the confrontation, all in the Sotho language (pronounced SOO-too), which Edna and Koos speak fluently.
Mashobene appeared to hold his ground for a while and then
to back down. Maybe all he had to do was make his point.

Koos and Edna met when she was a teacher at the primary
school in Middelpoort, a town of broad streets, neat houses
with flower gardens, and a mill on the main street where
people bring their maize to be ground. Edna grew up in
another part of the Free State where her family farmed, and
she is used to the life.

Koos will not allow his female guests to lounge around the
pool in scanty swimsuits when Black male workers are around,
for fear it will "upset" the men. He and Edna rarely relax
when Blacks can see them, for he senses their resentment
that *Baas* can take time off. The van der Merwes look forward
to Christmas, when they give the servants a three-day holiday and give themselves one as well.

Koos is a deacon in the Dutch Reformed church where
they attend services every Sunday, and Edna belongs to a
group of women who meet once a month in someone's home
and listen to an intellectually stimulating lecture presented
by one of the members. Made up of "the better women" of
Middelpoort, the group took their time in accepting Edna,
even though Koos is well known and well liked in the town.
Edna suspects jealousy and envy on the part of a couple of
the women who managed to keep her out for years. But now
that she is in, Edna is a dedicated member who invested a
great deal of effort in preparing her presentation when it was
her turn: she talked about gemstones of South Africa and
took her own collection of tigereye and other semiprecious
stones.

Edna is the kind of energetic woman who is enthusiastic
about everything that interests her, and she was definitely
enthusiastic about having a visitor from America. She tele-

phoned the local newspaper to suggest that an interview of the visiting writer would certainly be of interest to readers. But the editor, a member of the right-wing Conservative Party, was plainly hostile to the suggestion: "Tell the bloody American to get the hell out of here."

His reaction might have prepared Edna for what to expect when she contacted the principal of the high school. Could the American come by to visit, perhaps meet some students, sit in on some classes (even though she understood not one word of Afrikaans)? The response was essentially the same as the editor's. Edna demanded an explanation. This was what she got:

"These foreign journalists come to our school and act nice and go home and write lies about us. The woman will come here and see that more money is spent on White students than on Blacks, and she'll go back to America and write about that. You can't trust those bloody Americans. They all hate us."

The "bloody American" of course did not need to visit that or any other White school to be aware of the discrepancy between White and Black education; easily available statistics show that about eight times as much is spent on the education of a White child as is spent on a Black child. There is an average of one teacher for every eighteen White students, and one for every forty-three Blacks; most Black teachers do not have training even remotely equivalent to a White's.

Edna was furious and embarrassed. I was furious and amused. "Tell him I'll go home and write that the bloody Afrikaner bureaucrats are bloody rude," I said. I would have told him so myself, but Edna would not let me.

It was my idea to ignore the paranoid bureaucracy and simply stop by at the primary school where Piet's wife Peggy is a teacher. I could go with Piet, the racing-car enthusiast. What could be more natural than a husband stopping by his wife's classroom? And if he happened to have a friend along, what was wrong with that? I wanted to outflank the principal as much as I wanted to have a look at the school.

We drove slowly past the high school with a sign reading "Middelpoort Hoerskool" arching over the brick gateway and on to the *volkskool*, a modern brick building surrounded by landscaped lawns and flowerbeds. But it was Friday afternoon, and school had been dismissed early. Little round-faced blond Afrikaners with pale blue eyes, dressed in snappy blue blazers, lugging big leather satchels filled with books to take home for the weekend, waited outside for their mothers to pick them up.

I took a quick look inside the empty building. The classrooms open onto a stoep surrounding an inner courtyard, a metal footscraper mounted squarely in front of each door. Peggy has twenty-three pupils in her first-year class. Her room is high-ceilinged, bright and cheerful with pictures cut from magazines thumbtacked around the room to help the youngest pupils learn basic English vocabulary.

Pupils who live on farms outside of town are not bused to and from school but live in town in hostels, dormitories where from Monday through Friday they are looked after by houseparents. The primary children live in opposite wings of the same hostel, but teenage boys and girls are housed in separate buildings. Children learn independence quickly, taught by their houseparents to make their own beds and put away their own clothes, skills that have little use when they have servants to do everything for them at home on the weekend.

Koos had better luck with the White inspector of Black schools, who granted permission for me to visit the location outside of Middelpoort. Mr. Bothma called me "Madam" and accompanied me on the visit, not entirely convinced by Koos that I was not a Communist agitator sent to stir up trouble in his peaceful town. As we drove from his office down the bustling main street, I asked what the population of Middelpoort was.

"One thousand five hundred, Madam," he said.

"Somehow it seems like more than that," I commented.

"Oh, do you mean counting Blacks? There are seven or eight thousand of them, Madam."

IV

BLACK MIDDELPOORT

The Location

A wire fence separates two worlds, the White ▲▲▲▲▲ town from the Black location. Beyond the fence the roads are unpaved, muddy and rutted. Identical little boxes line up row upon row, the front door flanked by a window on each side, a forward-sloping tin roof. The government provides the houses, but some of the tenants have improved them. A few battered cars are parked here and there. Each house has a square of bare earth swept clean, a few strands of fencing, a bush or two. Clotheslines lace the yards. Little children playing in the dirt looked up to stare at the Mercedes; so did their mothers, chatting across the fence.

"Will you ask them if it's all right for me to take a picture?" I said to the school inspector.

He thought that was funny. "You don't ask these people for permission," he said with a chuckle. "If you want a photograph, you just take it."

I am not much of a photographer, but in my trips to other parts of the world I had learned that one always asks permission. That courtesy did not seem to apply here. With sign language (smile, point, wave camera) I negotiated with the women myself.

Built in 1980, the school is laid out in the style that prevails throughout the country: one-story brick buildings with classroom doors opening onto a roofed verandah, surrounding a rectangle of brown grass.

The high-school principal, a distinguished-looking Black man in his fifties who spoke excellent English, seemed proud to show off his school, and the inspector, apparently convinced by my naïve behavior that I was not dangerous, allowed me to go with him unchaperoned.

In a home-economics classroom equipped with shiny white stoves, thirty girls were rounding up the ingredients to cook mealie pap. They stopped dead at the appearance of a White visitor, but in a second the teacher had them shaped up: "Good morning, Madam!" She explained that I had come all the way from America to see their school "Ooooohhhh!" they gasped and dissolved into giggles.

"Perhaps you would like to say something to the class?" the teacher suggested politely.

"I bring you greetings from the children of the United States, who send you their best wishes," I said and hoped it was true. They smiled brilliant smiles and applauded.

The boys' woodworking shop was not in session, but the principal made sure I admired the well-kept lathes and rows of polished tools hung on pegs. In biology class ("Good morning, Madam!"), the instructor, a well-dressed man in a V-neck sweater with an animal symbol, continued his explanation of astigmatism, using a model eye to demonstrate.

On the way to the next classroom I heard singing. It was easy to find the source, a music class where the students were singing four-part harmony, using a system of musical notation that I did not understand. Following the teacher's pointer, they sang a progression of chords. The results were beautiful, and it was only an exercise.

Everyone—at least the teachers—seemed to expect me to say or do something. I stuck to my "Greetings from the Children of America" speech, expanded in the English class to urge them to read. There was no chance for conversation or questions; I was strictly a tourist-observer.

The next stop on the tour was a primary school run by the Catholic church. But the classrooms were empty; everybody was next door in the church for the midweek service. We arrived in time to hear several hundred children singing the Lord's Prayer at the top of their lungs. There was no accompaniment; a woman in the congregation started off, and the children joined in, in harmony.

A chain link fence surrounds the government primary school, and someone had to come and unlock the gate for us. It was a sharp contrast to the high school. The buildings seemed more run-down, the classrooms shabbier. The teachers were poorly dressed. The principal was missing most of his front teeth. There was a look of privation here that I had not observed in the high school, and I asked the inspector why this was so.

"It has to do with the teachers," he said. "Those in the high school have had more training, they are more highly qualified, and therefore they are better paid." His explanation may have accounted for the shabbier clothes and the poorer dental care, but it did not really explain to me why the high school measured up well against some in the United States while the primary school reeked of poverty.

They wanted to sing for me. While I watched a classroom of youngsters being taught to write Zulu, older pupils shuffled desks in another classroom. Some fifty students crowded in. Their leader tapped her red suede boots and gave them a pitch, and they launched into a two-part song. The girls took the lead and the boys responded in a harmonizing bass, swaying and stamping.

"Zulu wedding song," the principal explained, grinning his gap-toothed smile, and led me to his office to sign the official guest book.

No one knows precisely when the first Black tribes arrived in southern Africa. They migrated from central Africa to escape pressure of population growth and violence among warring tribes, in search of space, peace, and grass for grazing their cattle.

Most scholars divide Blacks of South Africa into groups based on the language they speak. The languages are known collectively as Bantu, a word meaning "the people" that has taken on a derogatory sense when applied to an individual. (It is insulting to call a Black person a Bantu or a Kaffir.) Although there are a number of recognized languages and many more dialects, the four most often used are Zulu, Xhosa, Sotho, and Tswana, spoken by about 90 percent of the total Black population. The Zulu are the largest tribe. Because of Middelpoort's location, both Sotho and Zulu live in the area, speaking their own language and maintaining their own traditions. All of the Blacks on the van der Merwe farm are Sotho.

It is clear that Black and White cultures are as different as black and white. Lack of understanding between the two races can often be traced to two opposing value systems. One is rooted in the competitiveness of European civilization that emphasizes the importance of the individual, the other in the African civilization that focuses on cooperation and community.

In Black tribal life, family is everything. Blood ties and marriage ties determine who you are and what you do. Marriage is the way by which a person achieves recognition as an adult. Before they can marry, boys and girls in areas where tribal life is still strong go through a period of preparation and a ceremony that confirms that they are ready for the responsibilities and privileges of adulthood. Each tribe has its rules for who may marry whom. In some tribes, people marry only within their own tribe; in others, they must marry people outside their tribe.

Status changes as a person grows up and grows older. Babies who are still being nursed are not blamed for their behavior, and since mothers nurse their infants until they are three or four, little children are hardly ever punished. Once they are weaned, though, they are expected to behave. Puberty is another major step. With marriage and the birth of the first child, men and women become adult members of the tribe. A man may have as many wives as he can support. Children are a sign of a woman's fertility and a man's power and wealth. A child has many "fathers" and "mothers," all ranked according to seniority. This network includes all the natural father's other wives, his brothers and their wives, and all of the natural mother's sisters. To Whites accustomed to the nuclear family, this is a strange idea.

African religions are more concerned with humankind than with the universe, with relationships among kin than with a supernatural being. A man reveres his ancestors and anticipates being revered by his descendants after his own death. Whites often dismiss the non-Christian beliefs of Blacks as superstitious mumbo jumbo.

Black economic philosophy, based on subsistence—having just enough—is at odds with the White European notion of production for profit. In a traditional tribal village each household produced only what it needed; a big family obviously needed more than a small one. But the idea of producing more than it needed and selling the surplus to someone else at a profit was a foreign concept. This may explain why

Isaac, Koos's farm manager, refused to take on more responsibility in return for higher wages; perhaps he felt that he had enough, and that having more was not worth the time and effort it would cost him. It may also explain why Koos's workers spend their money as fast as they earn it; saving for a "rainy day" or even for a luxury is simply not part of the culture, although Koos does his best to *make* it part.

The clash of values was apparent the first time the Whites encountered the Blacks in the 1770s, when the *trekboers* met the Xhosa, related to the Zulu. The Xhosa had no written language, while the *trekboers* carried their Dutch Bibles. The Xhosa knew nothing about the wheel, but in another couple of generations the Boers would be creaking across the country in ox wagons. Their political thinking was different, too: the Afrikaners' roots were in Europe, a part of the world where national boundaries were important, if only for violating them. The Xhosa had never heard of such a thing, and so it meant nothing to them when the government drew lines designating areas for specific groups of people in the eastern part of the Cape Colony. Perhaps most important, the deeply religious but narrow-minded Whites saw the Blacks as heathens who fought among themselves and represented the forces of evil in the world.

Whites today of both English and Afrikaner backgrounds seem to have little more understanding of Blacks than their ancestors did. What is clear is that they *think* they do. And they know that they are in charge, a small minority dominating a large majority.

In a bookstore in Johannesburg I picked up a pamphlet titled *Zulu Vocabulary and Phrase Book*, described as "simple sentences for use in the home and garden and on other occasions." It was a list of imperatives, orders for a White boss to give to a Black servant: *Take off your hat. Come at once when the bell rings. Prepare the food to be cooked. When you wash up, begin with the glasses. When you have done the glasses, wash the cups. Bring my tea early in the morning. When you have swept the house, take water and soap and wash the floor. Clean the boots in the morning after sweeping the kitchen and lighting the fire. Be respectful. . . .*

I think it would be easier to make my own tea and wash my own floor than to learn the complicated Zulu phrases. But I am not South African, and I do not really know how I would behave.

Initiation School

Petro Malan (pronounced mah-LAHN), Koos's sister, spoke Sotho before she learned Afrikaans. Her nursemaid talked to her in Sotho. The Black children she played with around the farm spoke nothing but Sotho. Like most Whites who grew up on farms, living among Blacks, she spoke the African language fluently, with all its subtleties and nuances.

Petro volunteered to use these skills to get me into an initiation school that prepares girls for marriage and adulthood. A farmer on the far side of Middelpoort had permitted a couple of the women who work for him to take a handful of adolescent girls to a secluded spot on the veld for a period of time, traditionally three months. It was all right with him, he said, if we went to see them. The trick was to make it all right with *them*.

Koos dropped us off with Petro's maid, Sophie, at a cluster of houses on the farmer's property. Koos was then chased off; males are not allowed anywhere near the "hiding." Sophie took us to her friend, a pregnant young woman whose dark face was coated with a light brown clay as a beautifier. The friend took us to her mother, Angelina. We crawled through a barbed-wire fence and followed Angelina down a dusty path through stubbled mealie-land toward a *spruit*, or spring. In traditional tribal villages initiation schools were held in a hut out on the veld, but this shallow ravine was probably the best they could do in an Afrikaner farming community.

Two women came to meet us. "That one has Bushman blood," Petro whispered, indicating a wizened old lady, her bony face crinkled and creased. The other was much younger and much fatter. Both wore colorful knitted caps, layers of faded cotton dresses, and blankets wrapped around their hips and pinned at the waist with huge safety pins. They were barefoot and had scarcely two dozen teeth between them.

Petro wheedled, joked, and cajoled the women. She was answered with laughter and smiles and arms folded firmly across chests.

"They're reluctant to let you come," Petro explained. Without understanding the reason for their reluctance, I tried some of Petro's smiling and head-bobbing to convey that I was a friend, not an intruder. As it turned out, it was because I had come too soon; the girls were only two weeks into their training for womanhood. It would be better if I came back at the end, in a couple of months. We proceeded a few steps and stopped for more wheedling, more joking, more laughter. A few more steps were won. Finally I was allowed to approach the edge of the ravine.

There were nine large bundles on the ground; it took me a moment to realize those were nine girls curled up under thick blankets. The skinny old woman and the fat young one called out to them, and nine heads poked out shyly from under the blankets. Their faces were smeared with grease mixed with charcoal. At another order from the women, the girls rose and dropped their blankets. Short skirts made of cowhide were wrapped and fastened in front, and they wore thick rope belts low on their hips. (Girls whose families can-

64

not afford real leather use blankets muddied to resemble hide, Petro said.) They were bare-breasted.

At a command from their teachers the girls formed a line and began a repetitious chant, one leading off, the others singing in response, stamping in time to their singing. Once over their self-consciousness, they kept it up, singing and singing—but softly, so that no men who might have ventured into the area could hear them. Songs of welcome and gladness, Petro said.

For the next ten weeks the girls would camp out in the open, learning what it is to be a Sotho woman. They are supposed to be virgins when they go for training, soon after their first menstruation, but those rules have been relaxed. They ranged in age from about fifteen to eighteen, well past the onset of their first periods, and one would guess from their pendulous breasts that some had already borne and nursed a child. Apparently it had become a practical matter, of when the White farmer agreed to give their teachers time off to hold the school.

At the end of their training, they would smear white clay over their bodies. Then they would wash off the clay and discard the leather skirts and belts, symbolizing their old lives. They would put on a tiny apron called a *motolo* and beads to indicate their readiness for marriage, and they would take new names.

Meanwhile the young men of the tribe must also go through an initiation, the chief feature of which is circumcision. They are required to endure this painful procedure, done with an assegai, a reed, or sometimes a surgical knife, without whimpering or crying, either during the surgery or during the painful healing process. They too live off in a secluded place for three months and coat their bodies in white clay. Customs differ among the tribes, but each has some variation of these rites of passage.

The girls hiding under the blankets near the *spruit* outside Middelpoort would, at the end of their seclusion, be available for marriage. The young men of the area would look them over and make their choices, and the negotiations would begin. The man would speak to his father, and his family would offer *lobola*, a bride-price. In return her family must provide the things necessary to establish a home. The discussion goes on until the families agree, and the marriage takes place after a child has been conceived or born, proof of fertility.

On the way back Petro described a custom that relates to the way the Sotho deal with the death of a child. They believe that the ancestors must have looked with disfavor on the child or were somehow displeased. So the next child born to the parents is known as "the dog" and treated in a very offhand way, as though it is of no importance, hoping that the ancestral spirits will overlook it and spare its life. The child designated as the dog is marked, its head shaved except for a little tail at the back of the neck that is plaited and twisted with beads. The life of "the dog" is difficult; people go out of their way to ignore it. This hard time lasts until the child is ready for initiation school, when an older man in the family—usually an uncle, but a brother in a pinch—comes to cut off the tail.

Petro recalled a girl who for some reason had no older man to do this for her. Her mother secretly cut off the tail, and the two pretended that a spirit had come during the night and done it. The ordeal was over, and the girl could go to initiation school.

Africans have a rich lore of spirits and sprites, elfin creatures. One called Tokolosche is about two feet tall and covered in gray fur with a gray beard that hangs down to his knees; a pebble that he keeps clenched in his fist or in his cheek makes him invisible. Tokolosche is a water sprite who lives near rivers, and he is so much of a troublemaker that

Blacks build their kraals on hilltops to keep away from him. As a further precaution many people raise their beds on stacks of bricks so Tokolosche can't reach them. And one White man told me that after he posted a sign on his gate reading "Tokolosche Security System," thievery around his house stopped immediately.

I had a lot of questions about all of this, but Petro brushed me off. "It's just silly superstition," she said. "Can you imagine giving these people the vote?"

Home on the Veld

A house with thick walls was built of clay bricks dug with a spade when the ground was wet. The string of rooms are not connected; two have thatched roofs blackened with soot, two are roofed with corrugated metal weighted down with rocks to keep them from blowing away. The doorways are low, the windows small. Geometric patterns have been scratched into the wet mud plastered on the end walls, and the front of the house is decorated with a checkerboard pattern of black, white, gray, and orange squares. The black comes from battery acid, the white from lime, gray is a mixture of the two, and the orange color is a local clay. The wash hangs in a colorful line on the wire fence across the road. A flock of Muscovy ducks huddles in a narrow strip of shade. The bare dirt yard in front of the house has been swept with a short-handled grass broom—the kind made and used by all the women—to form a pattern of arcs. I hated to walk on it and spoil the design.

The house is immaculate. The dirt floors have been smeared with dung liquefied with water that dries to a hard finish; some floors are also covered with linoleum, cracked and broken but well scrubbed. A collection of pretty china is displayed on shelves across one end of the room. Shiny pots and pans are stacked on top of the stove. A curtain at the opposite end marks off the sleeping area furnished with a European-style bed, chest of drawers, and wardrobe. The bed is covered with a crocheted spread and decorated with a stuffed animal and a doll in a fancy dress. The doll is White.

The sixty-five-year-old woman who shares this house proudly showed me her stack of dung cakes. There are no trees on the veld, no wood to burn; fuel for cooking and heating comes from mealie cobs or from cow dung, of which there is no shortage. The dung is collected and stored for a while to allow the dung beetle to work through it, removing disease-breeding bacteria. Then the women mix the dung with water, work it with their feet, form it into cakes, and mark the cakes with their own handprint signature, so that each woman knows which cakes are hers. The top of the heap is protected from rain with a layer of unprocessed dung. The dung burns to a clean ash.

What she needs here, one of the women told Edna, who translated for me from Sotho, is a chicken run. Since she has no husband to build it for her, four times she had invited several men from the area to come and construct it; in return she treated them to sorghum beer. Sorghum is an important crop here, because it is extremely resistant to drought and can stand a hotter climate than mealies. It has many uses, including thatching material, and it is traditional for making beer. Four times the men appeared, drank the home brew from calabashes cut from gourds, and left without doing a thing about the chicken run. Next week she planned to try again, this time with a different group of men.

Easter, the van der Merwes' "cook boy," lives in a house decorated with large-scale supergraphics much more elaborate than the checkerboard design. His family has the luxury of a separate bedroom and a large white refrigerator in a place of honor in the lounge, but his wife does most of the family cooking outside behind a screen of woven reeds. There is a metal bucket in which to burn the dung cakes and big three-legged iron cooking pots in the outdoor kitchen.

There was a water tap in the yard but no toilets visible, even of the outdoor privy kind. "Where do they go?" I asked Edna. "Out there," she said, waving her hand at the empty fields.

Koos, who has lived his entire life on this farm, has never been inside the homes of his workers. Edna has visited a few times. They told me about a neighboring farmer who put up houses for his workers according to his own notions. But the housing turned out to be unpopular with the residents, who showed their displeasure by leaving them undecorated. They have cement floors, for one thing, rather than dung-coated dirt. Cement is much colder in winter, but it has a further disadvantage: it is impossible to bury the placenta under the bed after a birth, which Blacks believe is necessary to continued fertility. Those unpopular houses also have large windows; most rural Blacks prefer tiny windows, fearful that evil spirits may enter.

"Blacks don't want to live on the farms anymore, and that's why they haven't decorated those houses," Edna said. "The Blacks around Middelpoort want to move off the farms and onto the location near town. They think they'll earn higher wages there. What they find out is that the higher cost of living offsets any increase in wages. Then they wind up worse off than they were before, with a White farmer taking care of them." Edna shook her head in resignation. "But you can't tell *them* that," she said.

The Farm School

On a shady patch of ground between the main house and the road to town stands a two-room schoolhouse for the workers' children of Kaalplaats. Two children who have misbehaved stand under a tree, giggling. An ancient bicycle leans against the fence.

Koos is paid a token of thirty rands a year as "manager" of the farm school, but he has never been inside the building. Two young men teach the classes. Victor, Easter's son, instructs the four primary grades, and Korrie teaches the next four grades. Both have a Standard Eight diploma plus a year of teacher's training, the equivalent of an eleventh-grade education. There are similar schools every few miles, and the pupils play rival farm schools at soccer, matches that sometimes go on for days.

Pupils may go to the high school on the location in town if they wish, but Koos does not encourage them. "More education will only make them dissatisfied with farm life," he said. "Leaving home means they will not fit in when they come back." He cites his own experience as a young man, when he left Middelpoort to study agriculture at Stellenbosch. "I had lost touch by the time I came home. I was no longer one of the 'locals' and I had a hard struggle finding my way back in."

Children sitting on molded plastic chairs share polished wooden desks on tubular metal legs. There are about three dozen children from six to ten years old in the lower grades. The age range of children in the upper grades is much wider. Here as elsewhere in South Africa, as Black children get older they are able to attend classes less regularly and may be in their upper teens before they finish even eight years of school. Nearly all of them wear uniforms, white shirts and black skirts and pants, inevitably dusty.

Victor and Korrie looked somewhat nervous at the arrival of White visitors—this is the first time Edna has been to the school—but the children were stiff with fear. Korrie speaks English with a heavy accent, and although this is solidly Afrikaner territory, the children are instructed in English. This was a big issue in Black education a few years ago, and,

70

in fact, the trigger that set off the Soweto uprising in 1976. Afrikaans is seen as the "language of the oppressor." As a result, most Blacks choose to be taught in English, although they will rarely have a chance to use it in the rural areas.

Today, though, was Korrie's chance to show off his pupils, and he selected one of the girls to give a recitation. I was not able to understand one word of it, although occasionally I did recognize that some strange version of my language was being rattled off at high speed. I did not want to embarrass any of us by asking Korrie what it was that she had recited.

"Now Caroline," Edna said cheerfully, "you just go ahead and ask these children anything at all you want to know."

Thirty-six wide-eyed faces stared at me. At that moment we were all rescued by the arrival of Victor, who wanted us to come next door to hear his children sing. Victor had his singers packed in tight rows against the chalkboard. By now I knew that unaccompanied choral singing is a custom in Black schools. Although Victor pitched the tune a bit too high for their full-voiced style of singing, it was lovely. But I did not realize until they finished and we were applauding that they had been singing in English.

Later Koos asked how the visit had gone. Edna said, "Koos, you should have it painted."

"Too late," Koos muttered. "She'll go home and write that our farm school needs painting. We should have done it before she got here."

Dinner at Kaalplaats

On my last night in Middelpoort, Edna invited members of the family to come by for dinner to answer any questions that I might have. But I never got to ask them.

Besides Koos and Edna, there were Koos's sister Petro, her son Piet the car racer, and Piet's wife Peggy, the teacher.

Easter was outside grilling thick lamb chops from a freshly slaughtered sheep, Koos broke out his best South African wine, and I was urged to eat my fill of biltong. But "drinkies" lasted a long time, as usual (White South Africans have a reputation for heavy drinking), and real feelings that had been cloaked in polite language for several days now broke through the smooth surface of my visit.

"Our mistake," Petro said, "was to urbanize the Blacks before they were civilized." Their definition of "civilized" seemed to mean adopting the White culture, including Christianity and other Western customs. "All the Blacks want to go to the cities because they think they can earn so much more money there. They don't realize it will take all they earn just to survive. But," she added, "you can't tell them that."

"Black men who leave their homes in the country to work in the mines around Johannesburg have made a choice, and if that means they must live in men's hostels, that is their decision," Piet said. "Nobody is forcing them to do it."

"But they get home to see their families only once a year," I protested. "Shouldn't they be allowed to take their families with them?"

"Their tribal rivalries are so strong that the men fight among themselves constantly in the hostels," Piet said. "It would mean constant violence if the wives and children were there, too."

I didn't follow that reasoning; I said I thought having wives and children around would be a stabilizing influence.

"They don't fancy family life the way we do," said Peggy. "They want to have wives and children all over the place."

"You can't let the Blacks all move to the city just because they want to," Edna said. "There aren't enough jobs. There probably won't even be enough water for everyone in a few years."

"They're like children, really," Petro said. "You have to understand Black psychology. You can't simply accuse one of them of stealing, even if you know they did. You just say that something is 'missing' and ask them to help find it." She described the time her good china was disappearing piece by piece. When she asked her maid to help her find it, the china began to reappear piece by piece—quite dirty, too, Petro claimed, because it had obviously been hidden in the maid's pile of dung cakes.

"More like savages than children," Piet amended. "Idi Amin is your typical Zulu." Amin was the ruthless Ugandan who subjected his people to a reign of terror during his tyranny over that East African nation. Piet told the story of King Moshoeshoe, the Black chieftain, whose father was killed and eaten by six warriors of another tribe. "That made the father part of the six who ate him, and the six cannibals then had to be protected until they died naturally. Only then could the father's spirit be put to rest. That's how Blacks think."

"Our mistake," said Peggy, "was to give medicine to the Blacks that reduced the infant mortality rate and extended their lives. That has allowed Blacks to outbreed Whites and outnumber us." (The infant mortality rate among Blacks in South Africa remains extremely high.)

"Our mistake was to put apartheid on the lawbooks," Edna added. "You have apartheid in the United States. You keep Blacks separate, and they are a minority, not like here. It's having it on the lawbooks that has the whole world against us."

"Our mistake," said Piet finally, "was not to kill them all off, as you did your Red Indians."

Fortunately at that moment Easter wheeled in a platter of sizzling chops and a half dozen other dishes, and there was something to do besides talk politics.

PART THREE

White on White:
English and Afrikaners

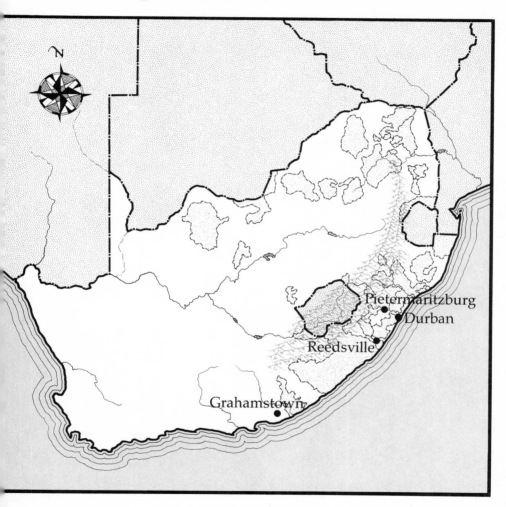

V

GRAHAMSTOWN

Blame it on the French.

▲ ▲ ▲ ▲ ▲ Inspired by the French Revolution, the Dutch in Holland replaced their monarchy with a republic, and in 1795 the prince of Orange, mindful of what happened to the heads of French royalty, made a quiet getaway to England. The Dutch ruler asked his British friends to take over his colonial possessions and look after them until he was restored to the throne. The British agreed and that same year sent some soldiers down to occupy the Cape Colony. The Cape was returned to the Dutch in 1803, but three years later the British were back. In 1814 their presence was made official and permanent.

At first the Boers were unconcerned. They saw themselves as Afrikaners, not as Dutchmen. They had resented the heavy hand of the Dutch East India Company, and it seemed to them that English rule could be no worse. But they were wrong. The British soon made themselves immensely unpopular with the Afrikaner farmers on a number of issues.

In 1812 the British established a circuit court to hear complaints lodged by Coloured slaves against their masters. The British viewed this as an attempt to extend protection of the law equally to all inhabitants of the Cape Colony, but the Boers saw it as an intrusion and resented it. One farmer who refused to appear in court to answer charges was killed by soldiers; when five of his neighbors protested they were arrested and sentenced to hang. Five Boers were lined up on the gallows, the boxes were kicked from beneath their feet, but only one man swung. The ropes around the necks of the other four snapped. Witnesses saw the broken ropes as a miracle and begged for clemency for the four survivors, but the British executioner hauled the condemned men back up and hanged them properly. Slachter's Nek, where the hanging took place, is a name that can still trigger anti-English bitterness in Afrikaners.

Another issue was language. From the beginning the British gradually eliminated Dutch from the schoolroom and the courtroom, and in 1828 English became the official language of the Cape Colony.

The British halted the importation of slaves in 1807, and in 1834 they abolished slavery altogether, decreeing that all slaves in the British Empire were to be set free. The English government offered a small reimbursement to the slave owners, a fraction of the investment the slaves represented, but there was a catch: the farmers had to go to London to collect the reparation. Few could afford to do that; the loss of their slaves represented a loss of capital, and many farmers were wiped out financially.

In the meantime boatloads of English settlers had begun to arrive. At that time there were about 23,000 Whites in the Cape, virtually all Afrikaners. A few English had already settled in Natal, but the largest single immigration took place in 1820, when five thousand English immigrants landed in the eastern Cape and established homes there. Several years earlier the English governor had sent a colonel named Graham to establish a military outpost on the eastern frontier. The settlement that grew up around the post came to be known as Graham's Town. In 1819 Xhosas attacked the post and nearly wiped it out. The following year the civilians arrived and were given small holdings of land around Graham's Town. The presence of all those people discouraged further attacks.

Many of the original English settlers had been craftsmen and tradesmen, not farmers, and their first attempts to raise crops were a failure. Others switched to the more successful business of raising sheep; within a generation eastern Cape wool surpassed western Cape wine as the colony's primary export. Some abandoned farming entirely and moved into what by then was being spelled Grahamstown.

By the 1850s the British government in Cape Town was stretched too thin and in too many directions. They had annexed Natal in 1844. It was easier to let the Boers have their two republics, the Orange Free State and the Transvaal, deep in the interior. Then two events took place that brought those remote republics into the world spotlight and completely changed the course of history.

In 1868 children playing near the Orange River found some sparkly stones: diamonds. Almost immediately fortune hunters from all over the world began to pour into the Free State. This did not go unnoticed by the British, who now attempted to declare the diamond fields a crown colony. Having given the interior a second look, they decided to take it over after all. The Boers were infuriated, and when Britain annexed the Transvaal in 1877 these angry Afrikaners did not need much of an excuse to pick up their guns and fight. They found their excuse when the British seized one of the farmers' wagons for failure to pay taxes. The First Anglo–Boer War (also called the First War of Independence) ended with the surprising rout of superior British forces at the Battle of Majuba Hill in 1881. A few months later the Transvaalers got "qualified independence."

After diamonds: *gold*. The discovery in 1886 of one of the richest gold-bearing ridges in the world in the Witwatersrand (pronounced the *w*s like *v*s) turned the lonely veld of the Transvaal into hot property. The gold rush was on. Within a few years Johannesburg had popped up out of nowhere. Enter Cecil John Rhodes, an Englishman who had made a fortune in diamonds by the time he was twenty-one years old and then went into politics. Rhodes had become prime minister of the Cape Colony and found himself bucking up against Paul Kruger, the Afrikaner who had led the Transvaal to independence. Rhodes was determined to have a united southern Africa under British rule, and Kruger stood stubbornly in his way: on the one hand, British imperialism, and on the other, Afrikaner nationalism. War was inevitable, and on October 11, 1899, the Second Anglo–Boer War (Second War of Independence) broke out.

It should have been all over in a few months; the British said by Christmas. After all, they had a large, well-trained, well-equipped army (some accounts say 500,000 men, others 350,000) and the Boers only a rag-tag band of 60,000 at most, perhaps only 35,000, no uniforms, few arms, no supply system, no training. But the Boers had picked up hit-and-run guerrilla tactics from their Black adversaries, and they used these against the British. The fighting dragged on for thirty-two months instead of two. The British resorted to a scorched-earth policy, burning the Boers' farms—crops, livestock, homes—and carried their women and children off to concentration camps, where 26,000 of them died from disease epidemics. In the end the Boers had to bow to superior numbers, but not before they had killed some 5,000 British soldiers and lost about 3,700 of their own men.

The Treaty of Vereeniging promised the Boers self-government, and the British agreed not to give Blacks the right to vote in Boer areas but to let the local legislatures decide. The fighting stopped in May 1902, but the bitterness persisted. Afrikaners had to accept the reality that they were British subjects, and they could not erase the memory of the women and children who died in the camps.

The Union of South Africa was formed in 1910, a self-governing dominion of the British Commonwealth. National leaders on both sides made reconciliation a top priority: the British victory was final, and it was time to blend the best of both English and Afrikaner cultures to create a united White people. But it has not worked quite that way. The Second Anglo–Boer War, like the Great Trek, is part of the history and folklore of Afrikanerdom, and the split is still there.

Geoff and Carol Cooper

Students at private boarding schools at Grahamstown, Geoff and Carol stayed behind to finish their education when their English-background parents emigrated to the United States to work for a large corporation. They took me to see the 1820 Settlers' Monument on the outskirts of Grahamstown. It is built on Gunfire Hill, where there used to be one of a series of signal towers stretching to the Fish River. The design is contemporary, preformed concrete and yellowwood, but the monument is functional, built to house conference centers and a theater and auditorium. From there we could look out over Grahamstown.

The prosperous center of a thriving farm area, Grahamstown is a noted educational center and the home of Rhodes University, thanks to the diamond magnate who also established the Rhodes Scholarships to Oxford University in England. There are a number of "colleges," as private boarding high schools are called. Beyond the town with its handsome school buildings, playing fields, expanses of trees and lawns, and bristle of church steeples (there are forty churches), lies the Black township known as Fingo. Grahamstown is a backwater, isolated from the energy of Cape Town and Johannesburg, but with its own festering wounds. It was Geoff's idea that we come down from this ivory tower and drive along the N2, the main highway from Port Elizabeth to East London, through Fingo.

We passed the streets to the university and the main street with its famous old churches, through a deteriorating commercial area and into the township. A Casspir was parked along the road, which was scattered with loose stones. It was Sunday and the place was crowded. I was uneasy, not sure whether all those people were simply enjoying the fine spring day or were about to pick up some of those stones and start hurling them at us.

Geoff pointed out the water taps—a pipe in the ground with a faucet—to which everyone in the area must go for all their water (there is no indoor plumbing here), and the miserable houses which Geoff said are on "time-share," meaning that families take turns using the houses to sleep, on eight-hour shifts. Carol told the story of one of the Black maids at her school who had stumbled in that morning after a sleepless night. Her next-door neighbor's house had been burned down the night before by *tsotsis*—hooligans—and her eyes were smarting with tear gas used by the police to control the crowd.

Who is to be feared more in Fingo (or in any Black

township)—the *tsotsis* or the police? Thugs use tough measures to enforce a boycott of White businesses in Grahamstown, forcing residents to buy only at Black shops in Fingo,
where prices are much higher. In other townships Blacks
violating the boycott have been forced to drink oil or deter-
gent purchased in White stores; some have died. Carol says
that the Black security men at her school who used to go
home late after locking up the dormitories and other buildings had been brutally beaten for violating the township curfew. Now the girls do their own locking up, and the security
men are sent home early. Some say that the presence of the
police incites trouble, but many others argue that the police
provide some kind of law and order and give Black citizens
a chance for a safe night's sleep.

The week before I came to Grahamstown there had been
an incident at Rhodes University, reported in the *Cape Times*:

POLICE CHARGE ON RHODES CAMPUS. Twenty Rhodes
University students and two academics were arrested,
and a number of protesters slightly injured, yesterday
when police with quirts [short whips or sjamboks]
charged about 300 demonstrators on the campus.

Police said the order to charge was given after stones
were thrown at them by protesters who ignored an
order to disperse. However, students and lecturers
denied that stones were thrown and said the protesters had retreated in response to the order.

The clash came after a day of protest on the campus
against the banning of the Congress of South African
Students last week.

The article went on to describe specific incidents: a professor
hit in the face after he was arrested, three women students
punched and kicked by the police, a male student protesting

the assaults on the women who was then himself assaulted and arrested. It cited a police spokesman's statement asking that complaints be brought to police stations where sworn affidavits would be taken, and thorough investigations initiated. This kind of statement provokes cynical laughter from people who know the police are not inclined to investigate their own violence.

Geoff was outraged by the incident. He said the police brought with them sacks of rocks to plant on the demonstrators in order to have an excuse to move in with their sjamboks and tear gas. "It was no riot," Geoff insisted. "It was a silent demonstration and very peaceful. I was there."

Fitzhugh McCarthy

Graying at the temples, handsome and slightly rumpled, Fitz is the kind of teacher who appeals to girls. There is something romantic and faintly tragic about him as well. Carol had been quoting him frequently, and she was delighted when he invited us for tea. Geoff admires him too but calls him an "irritable Irishman" and begged off to study.

Fitz is a recent immigrant from a country to the north that was called Rhodesia until 1980. Originally named for Cecil Rhodes, it was renamed Zimbabwe. People who moved to South Africa from Zimbabwe when the minority White government there was taken over by a Black majority are sometimes referred to as "When we's"—as in "When we lived in Rhodesia. . . ."

Leaving Rhodesia/Zimbabwe was painful for Fitz, as it is for anyone who leaves a beloved country and a way of life. At first he and his family emigrated to Canada, but he found that he was miserably homesick for southern Africa. "I lay in bed at night, sleepless, and yearned for the primitiveness of Africa," he said, "where rhinos crash through the bush and elephants trumpet, and I couldn't bear to be away from that kind of land."

So the McCarthys returned to Africa and settled in Grahamstown. "When we lived in Rhodesia," he said, "I cherished the notion that Blacks and Whites would forge a union, combine the best of both cultures, live side by side in a harmonious multiracial society. Now nationalism on both sides has torn all that apart. And it's tearing it apart here, too."

Fitz's son, Ben, seventeen, is a classmate of Carol's. "Ben is very conservative," Carol ventured. "When we talk about it we always get into an argument, because he has no sympathy whatsoever for the Black position. He says they should be quelled, put down."

"That's because he doesn't know any Blacks," Fitz explained. "He didn't grow up with them as I did. In Rhodesia there was a chance to know Black people intimately. And so Ben sees it only as a matter of power—and power belongs to the man who carries the gun. As long as Whites have guns and Blacks don't, Ben argues that the Whites will maintain control."

"What do you think?" I asked him.

He sighed a long sigh. "I honestly don't know. I am determined to stay here now, whatever happens. It was probably a mistake to come back. I simply cannot leave Africa, but I'm preparing my children so that they can leave, if it comes down to that."

"Ben doesn't think it will."

"He could be wrong. Most of the students here simply don't want to hear about it, don't want to deal with what's happening. They think it's a temporary maladjustment."

The next day I sat in on Fitz's history class. It meets in a modern brick building with mutilated old desks. There were about twenty girls from Carol's school and a smattering of boys from Geoff's; the two have separate campuses but share some of their classes. The content of the class is laid out in a government syllabus, although this is a private school. What is taught is closely controlled.

Carol had been shocked by her idol's display of emotion over the teacups. She knew him as a good teacher, an interesting lecturer who sometimes departs from the syllabus to draw out the students' feelings but never expresses his own. "He can't say what he really thinks about what's going on in South Africa," she explained. "If he did, and it was at odds with government policy, someone could report him. He'd lose his job. He could end up in prison."

Now Fitzhugh McCarthy stood at a lectern, half-glasses sliding on his nose, shirttail working loose, and led the class through a fill-in-the-blanks recap of last week's unit on the Asians. This week the syllabus prescribed a lesson on "Coloureds."

"Who can define 'Coloured' for us?" Fitz asked, and when no one volunteered an answer he called on one of the girls. "Half-breeds between Black and White?" she suggested. Fitz had his work cut out for him to correct the misconception. He explained to them about the Khoisan—Hottentots and Bushmen—who mingled with Whites to produce Griquas, about the Cape Malays who are not Black African but Asian, and other combinations of White and non-White.

From there he launched into the political history of the Coloureds, beginning in 1910 with the Union of South Africa. In Cape Province the Coloureds were at one time enfranchised, allowed to vote, because "brown Afrikaners" were considered Western in culture and Christian in religion, unlike the Black heathen. Gradually their political position was eroded. Although legal efforts were made to retain their rights, the vote was taken away from them. During the period from 1951 to 1957 the Coloureds were removed from the political system, despite court fights aided by Jewish lawyers who, Fitz said, were often in the forefront of civil liberties.

"We need a great playwright to capture the great struggle of this period," he said.

The girls generally focused their attention on scribbling notes, but one boy asked challenging questions that no one else seemed to think of. As it turned out, Gerhardt was an exchange student from Germany. He asked about the reputation Coloureds have for being alcoholic; Fitz explained the old *dop* system that kept Coloured vineyard workers slightly fuzzy. But Fitz was not content to leave it at that. He described the reaction of men of low self-esteem, who drink to forget that they no longer feel like men. When Fitz mentioned that most Coloureds are members of the segregated Dutch Reformed church, Gerhardt asked how Coloureds could accept a religion that preached that racial mixing is a sin, when they are in fact the products of such mixing.

Then the German student asked, "What determines the percentage of non-White blood it takes to make someone Coloured?"

"If you can pass for White, you're White," Fitz said and listed some of the criteria: skin color, hair texture, the color of a woman's nipples, a line of hair on the buttocks, the moons on the fingernails—all completely unscientific but all used at some time for racial classification.

Fitz turned to me. "What does 'Coloured' mean in the United States?" he asked.

"It hasn't been used for years," I said. "It's considered a derogatory term. Now we say Black."

"But the C in NAACP?" he pressed, referring to the National Association for the Advancement of Colored People.

"We don't spell it out," I hedged.

"A governor of Mississippi used to say that NAACP stood for Niggers, Apes, Alligators, Coons, and Possums," he joked, but his joke sounded hollow.

Pettigrew House

Carol had obviously not chosen her school for the beauty of its uniforms. They are truly ugly: brown jumpers, short-sleeved white shirts, brown sweaters, brown knee socks, brown shoes, narrow beige sashes tied in back. Prefects—student leaders—get to wear green sashes and special badges.

The girls poured out of Pettigrew House looking like a flock of drab wrens. "Good morning, Mrs. Simms," they murmured to the snowy-haired housemother.

When I stopped by the dormitory on Sunday afternoon the scene was quite different, the girls' trendy clothes pretty much like those worn in high schools in the United States. Sunday afternoon is a time for entertaining visitors, primarily male, from other schools. A group of them sat stiffly on straight-backed chairs in the common room, watching television.

I went upstairs to snoop. The younger girls live six to a crowded, messy room, snuggled together like puppies, beds unmade, towels and clothes strewn everywhere. Some of the smaller rooms had no doors, only curtains hung in the doorways. In one room two Black girls sat knitting at opposite ends of a narrow bed. Rock music blared from a radio. On the landing stood the brass gong that regulates the girls' lives—clanging the signal to wake up, go to breakfast, go to class, eat lunch, end rest period, and so on.

While Carol and I waited for the housemother to come back so that I could be properly introduced, I lifted the edge of a towel that covered a large baking pan on a shelf in her office. There were stacks of sandwiches, yellow cheese on wholewheat rolls, oozing mustard. "What's *this*?" I whispered.

"Supper," Carol said. "Like to stay?"

Most of the girls of Pettigrew House go out for Sunday dinner, and so only a light meal is provided in the evening. I declined.

The Settlers' Inn

I thought of those sandwiches that night while I feasted on prawns at the Settlers' Inn—the only "international" hotel in town, Geoff told me, meaning that Blacks were permitted to stay there. Two Black men ate at the table next to mine, where I struggled with the prawns.

Meals were often a struggle for me in South Africa. I tried hard to follow that old rule, "When in Rome, do as the Romans do," including proper table manners. There is great emphasis in doing things *correctly* throughout South Africa, but manners are much more formal than they are in the United States. I was forever trying to figure out how to deal with the silverware. Once, in a restaurant noted for its good food and fine service, I stared in dismay at a table setting that included four knives and at least that many forks and spoons of various shapes and sizes to left and right of my plate, not counting a few more items arranged in front of my plate. I remembered my mother telling me to start from the outside and work toward the center, but she had not been a believer in the "Continental" style of eating—fork in the left hand, tines down, knife in the right as a pusher, none of that continual back-and-forth style favored by Americans. I ended up feeling awkward no matter which way I tried to eat. And now, in an international hotel in Grahamstown, I did not know what to do with half a dozen prawns firmly encased in their shells.

In my own home I would have attacked them like lobsters, but I was not sure that these fastidious English would not have gone after them with knife and fork. I tried that. One landed in my lap. I gave up and grabbed it. Moments later the waitress appeared with a fingerbowl. Had I committed a terrible gaffe by eating with my hands, and did the waitress bring the fingerbowl as an unspoken comment on my uncouthness? Or was I doing it right and the fingerbowl came as a matter of custom?

This was one of many small reminders that although I was hearing and speaking my own language (although with a different accent) and the cultures seemed similar if not identical, South Africa is in fact quite different from the United States.

When one of the Black men left the table next to mine, I gathered my courage and introduced myself to the one left. His name was Luke, he said, and he was a lighting technician with a crew from SABC-TV, the state-run television network, in Grahamstown to shoot a TV movie. There were thirty-five in the crew, he told me, including the White producer from England who was holding hands with a beautiful Coloured woman, permissible now that the ban against sexual mixing of the races had been lifted. Luke is from Johannesburg—"Where the real life is, not in this backwater." He grew up in Orlando, part of Soweto. "They call it a granny suburb," he said, "because it's such an old town."

I asked about his training. "I failed my matric in 1975. That was before the changes in education in 1976. You know something?" he said, cutting into a piece of beef. "Education for Blacks was terrible then. It's even worse now."

The phone in my room jangled late that evening. It was Roger, a salesman who had picked up my accent when he overheard me speaking to the desk clerk. "Can you come out to the lobby? I want to talk to you."

I threw on some clothes and stuck in my contact lenses. Roger had just wound up a long day with his clients—he represents a clothing manufacturer—and wanted to wind down over a cup of coffee with the traveling American.

"I suppose you want one man, one vote," he said, referring to a change in the current nonvoting status of Blacks. "You people won't be satisfied until you've turned the country over to the Blacks. Why are you all so fascinated with South Africa? Why don't your journalists focus their attention on the Middle East or Central America where the situation is *really* bad? Our Blacks are better off than those in any other country in Africa. Why *us*?"

Mr. Peterson

Three hundred girls in brown uniforms sat crosslegged on the bare floor of the assembly hall at seven-thirty in the morning, awaiting the entrance of headmaster Gregory Peterson. He swept in in a black academic robe, and they scrambled to their feet and chorused cheerfully, "Good morning, Mr. Peterson." The headmaster announced a hymn, and we staggered through words having to do with the strength to live courageously to the accompaniment of a piano played hesitantly.

Back down on the floor again we listened to Mr. Peterson address the matters of the day: awards for improvement, triumphs in hockey and tennis, thanks for cooperation during the current water shortage. (The reservoir for Grahamstown was at a fraction of capacity, something less than twenty percent, and students were limited to three showers a week, that water then recycled to flush the "loo.") A few teachers made announcements, everyone stood in respectful silence as teachers and headmaster filed out, and the rush was on to classes. I was on my way to meet Mr. Peterson before I left Grahamstown, and I caught up with Carol to give her an American-style hug.

"Do you understand now why Geoff and I wanted to come here to school, rather than go to school in the States?"

I had to confess that I did not. The formality is rather nice, the discipline is impressive, but I am used to a more casual lifestyle.

Carol and Geoff are obviously very proud of their schools. When their parents first moved to the United States, Carol and Geoff spent a couple of years in American schools, both public and private, and begged their parents to send them back to South Africa. They could not adjust to the casual American approach to education. It seemed undisciplined to them.

Schools operate with a formality that has not existed in the United States for a generation. *All* South African students wear uniforms, no matter how poor the school or impoverished the family. And in every classroom I visited, no exceptions, the entire class rose and in chorus greeted me and whoever was with me. Tradition is treasured, and discipline strictly maintained.

The grade system is different. The first year of school (children may start at age six, but seven is compulsory) is called "Sub A," the second "Sub B." Their third grade is known as "Standard One" and the standards go up to Ten, the equivalent of twelfth grade or senior in high school. Toward the end of Standard Ten, students take a series of written examinations established by the government called matriculation exams, which also serve as university entrance exams. The exams are sometimes referred to as "matrics," and Standard Ten students are also called "matrics." In

South Africa "college" means "private high school." One goes to university, sometimes called "varsity," after high school. In the United States university can be referred to as "school," (as in "Where did you go to school?" "Harvard.") but "school" in South Africa means high school or primary school.

Education for each racial group is controlled by a different ministry of the government. Every province has an education department that administers its own system of senior certificate examinations for students who have completed high school and either have finished their schooling or are going on for technical training. There are eight *technikons*, offering a combination of theory and practice similar to universities, and a number of technical colleges and institutes for Whites. Technical schools for Blacks, Coloureds, and Asians are, of course, separate.

The children are worried, Mr. Peterson said, about what their future will be, but they are more optimistic than the adults. I asked him how this worry is manifested. "By talking about it," he said.

This was not the impression I got from Fitzhugh McCarthy. I thought that if I were a student I would be more likely to express my worries to the romantic Fitz than to the proper ("Pompous," one girl said) Mr. Peterson. He had invited a political science professor from Rhodes as well as the local chief of police to come and talk to the students, so that they would hear both sides of the issue. "If they go to a liberal university," he said, "they'll get only one side."

Peterson described the girls' school and its male counterpart down the street as "very conservative and old-fashioned." The previous Saturday night all the Standard Nines and Tens had dressed up in long white dresses for a formal dance, an old, cherished tradition. When someone had suggested that

93

they might just want to wear jeans and skirts, she was roundly voted down.

About a third of his students are local, residents of Grahamstown and neighboring farms; a third come from other parts of South Africa; and a third are "exotics" like Geoff and Carol and the German boy in Fitz's history class, whose families live in other parts of Africa or even other parts of the world. People here tend not to move around much; the Pringles and the McNaughtons around Grahamstown are descendants of the 1820 settlers with those names.

"It's hard country," he said, "and survival has always been difficult. Students are stoic and assume that their 'tribe' will survive again." To outsiders, like me, that stoicism looks like arrogance.

Sitting in the morning assembly, I had estimated that about 10 percent of those little brown wrens were Black. "That is the maximum permitted by law," Peterson explained. "More than that and the school loses its government support, which would push the tuition beyond the reach of most families, Black and White." But there is a long waiting list of Blacks from well-to-do families (an almost infinitesimal fraction of the Black population), and the headmaster would like to boost that enrollment to something like 20 percent. "I want to prove that it can still be done with no sacrifice of quality."

Gregory Peterson is not the only White educator concerned with making top-notch education available to talented Blacks. Colleague Richard Todd (his real name; Peterson's name has been changed) was headmaster of the elite Hilton College in Pietermaritzburg, Natal. When the school hired him, Todd made it clear that he was committed to multiracial, multicultural education and not just the "White cream," which he described as "thick and rich." Todd's idea was to integrate gifted Black pupils into Standard Nine and Ten classes at Hilton.

After three years he had succeeded in bringing in only a dozen Black pupils. He had run up against the Old Boys— men who supported the school financially and called the tune—who were determined to keep Blacks out. Todd quit. With a donation of ten million rand from one of South Africa's largest corporations he started the school of his dreams.

In an interview in a South African business magazine, he explained his reasoning: "After all, 85% of Black teachers don't have matric [have not passed the Standard Ten examinations] and only 2% have degrees [from universities]." This means that even highly gifted Black students receive such a poor basic education that they have almost no chance of getting into a recognized university. He wants to catch bright pupils in their next-to-last year of high school and bring them up to university entrance level in two years. Todd sees himself as educating future leaders. Besides, he maintained, the government's failure to educate Blacks contributes to what he calls "escalating waves of unrest." The country cannot afford to waste the potential of talented Blacks, he argued, and then made the one point that might carry some weight: "Politically it would be extremely dangerous."

But sometimes giving a "White education" to a Black student creates problems of its own. Peterson told me the story of the Nganis, an upper-middle-class family, who are attempting to buy high-quality educations for their five children. The eldest son graduated from Geoff's school, but Roland did not do well enough on his matrics to be admitted to a White university. Instead he went to Ft. Hare, one of the Black universities. But he did not fit in there; he had too many White friends from his boarding-school days, and he could not share the anger the other Blacks focused on Whites. Finally he dropped out. Now the headmaster of the boys' school was trying to persuade Rhodes to accept Roland in spite of his poor showing on the matric. Roland's sister Darlene is a Standard Nine. Mr. Peterson was keeping his fingers crossed that Darlene would do well on her matrics.

As I was leaving, Mr. Peterson wrote the family's telephone number on a slip of paper. "Look up Mrs. Ngani when you get to Umtata," he said, where until then I had no contacts at all.

VI

REEDSVILLE

Hennie and Lucy Potgieter

Seven o'clock in the morning. The sun glit-
▲ ▲ ▲ ▲ ▲   tered on a heavy frost, and the hot-water
bottle I had taken to bed was cold as a stone. Draped in a
duvet, a down-filled comforter, I crept down the hall. Three
Black women, hair wrapped in headcloths that matched their
dresses, were on their hands and knees, scouring the wooden
floors of the old farmhouse. Hennie and Lucy Potgieter were
not up yet, but Hennie's work shoes, neatly shined, stood
outside their bedroom door. One of the maids stopped scrubbing when I appeared and hurried to the kitchen. When I
came back from the bathroom, a teatray was beside my bed.

By the time breakfast was served, the wooden floors
gleamed, all the furniture was back in place, and the women
were outside scrubbing the stoep, barefoot, kneeling on the
icy stone floor. "Spring cleaning?" I asked Lucy. She looked
surprised. "They do it every day."

97

The Potgieters live in a corner of Natal near a town I have renamed Reedsville. When the British annexed Natal in 1844, most of the Voortrekkers packed up and moved on, but some —like the Potgieters and the Steyns, Lucy's family—stayed on and farmed. Hennie owns four farms around Reedsville, running about thirteen hundred head of cattle, plus the sheep. Like most farmers in this area, he grows maize, South Africa's most important crop, cultivated on about 50 percent of the arable land. It is exported in addition to being the staple food of the majority of the population.

Natal is known as the Garden Province because of its subtropical climate—except in areas like Reedsville, where elevation sometimes keeps it wintry until November. Bananas grow along the coast, pineapples in the north. Sugarcane is an important crop, some grown under irrigation in the lowveld of Natal and the eastern Transvaal and most in the midlands where there is no danger of frost. About half of the sugar produced is consumed in South Africa, and half is shipped to overseas customers. The United States has been a big sugar buyer.

Lucy had driven out to intercept me along the highway from Reedsville and had led me over miles of corduroyed dirt roads; I followed the cloud of dust kicked up by her Mercedes, sliding around corners in my little rented car. Lucy is a pretty woman, blond and blue-eyed like many Afrikaners but finer boned than most. Hennie is a big, bearish man with a glittering gold tooth and a reputation for outspokenness that both amuses and annoys Lucy, who tries to calm him down while simultaneously egging him on. She dresses elegantly and always wears stockings and heels, because her husband does not like women in pants. There is no reason for her to wear jeans since she is not involved in farm labor and there are servants to do all the housework.

"The girls are my friends," she told me, referring to the

Black women in the kitchen. "I know about their troubles and they know about mine." Lucy operates a store for them, buying sugar, flour, and other staples at wholesale prices and adding on twelve percent for the GST (government sales tax) and eight percent for herself. The "girls" have begun to ask her to buy things for them, like cups and other household items, and this has brought them closer together. "They tell me about their children, and about the problems they have with their husbands."

About 150 Blacks live on Hennie's farms. The modified Cape Dutch house with scrolled gables and dazzling white-wash was Hennie's boyhood home. Two years ago electric lines were brought in, but the cooking is still done on a coal stove. Cozily decorated with antiques—an old wooden log hollowed out and once used for grinding mealie meal, brass buckets filled with dried flowers—the kitchen is cheerful but not built for efficiency or for a servantless housewife.

Like many farm wives Lucy lives an isolated life, a forty-five-minute drive from town and far from neighbors. Hennie is often away from early morning until late at night, and she complains that they have little time for intimate conversation. Even when they go away on holiday, as they did during the winter, they have trouble finding anything to talk about. So Lucy's main sources of intimacy and companionship are her "girls."

Lucy was curious about the lives of women in America. South African men are notoriously sexist and chauvinistic; the role of women and the relationship between the sexes lag about thirty years behind the United States. In the company of married couples I often felt that I had been transported back to the 1950s. A woman traveling alone in a foreign country, as I was doing, was unheard of. American women are considered "forward," "aggressive," and are not much liked; South African men are affronted by our freedom, and

99

South African women feel threatened. I dealt with sexism the same way I dealt with racism—by keeping my mouth shut and by moving on before the veneer of politeness had time to wear thin.

Lucy wishes she had a closer relationship with Hennie, although she confesses that she has never really been in love with him. Not long ago Hennie took a course on managing farm labor, even though he protested that he had been bossing "niggers" for years and had nothing to learn. But something apparently got through to him, and Lucy started noticing changes in his attitude, even toward her. He began to do thoughtful little things for her, like running her bath water, that he had never done before. The trouble was, it didn't last.

She has known him all her life—they grew up on neighboring farms—and began going out together when she was a teenager. He is nine years older. When she finished high school she tried nurses' training for a few months before she bowed to the inevitable.

"I always knew I would marry Hennie," she said.

"Even though you didn't love him?"

She shrugged. "We were neighbors. We understood each other."

Lucy describes herself as scatterbrained and overly emotional, disorganized, undisciplined, prone to depression. She complains that many of the "Reedsville crowd" are friendly one day and ignore her the next. Brought up in the Dutch Reformed church, she worries about her religion, which often makes no sense to her. "The rules are so confusing," she said. "I think you simply have to sort out what suits and forget the rest."

To keep herself occupied, when she isn't looking for ways to keep the servants occupied, Lucy makes pottery, which she sells through a shop in town. She and some friends operate a catering service, preparing a buffet of cold meats, little cakes, and other delicacies for weddings. The money she earns comes in handy for household expenses, for although the farms represent a large capital investment, there never seems to be money to fix up the house. She wants to modernize the kitchen, but Hennie claims they don't have the cash to do it.

Their children all live away from home. When they were young they went to school in Reedsville and came home only on weekends. Willem, the oldest, manages one of Hennie's farms and lives in a cottage on his grandparents' property. For a while Willem stayed out in the *jonkershuis*, but that did not work out. There was constant friction between father and son, and Lucy disapproved of Willem's lifestyle. A strapping man with yellow hair, Willem had brought a girl to stay with him over the weekend. Lucy was horrified. "The Bible says sex before marriage is a sin, and I told him that. He laughed at me." Willem is twenty-two and says that his sex life is his own business; his mother does not accept that.

Freddie, the younger son, is doing his military service. Lucy worries about him. She saw a huge change in Willem when he came home from the army, and she doesn't want to see that change take place in Freddie. Was it the change of a boy into a man? I asked. She shook her head. "Something in his eyes," she said. "It frightened me."

Kristin, sixteen, spends the week in Reedsville at the hostel. Her bedroom is a fluffy mixture of child and woman: giant dolls on her ruffled bed and sophisticated fashion posters on the wall. Kristin is obviously Hennie's favorite. He claims that she knows more about the stock than he does, and he is actually encouraging her to study animal husbandry at university.

"She has no interest at all in boys," Lucy said, and Hennie just laughed. "That's what she tells *you*." When she comes home for the weekend there are no parties to go to, no dances, no films (she pronounces it "fillums"). I wondered what it would be like for Kristin to go off to Stellenbosch and get a degree in animal husbandry and marry one of these Afrikaners—perhaps someone like her brother Willem—and settle down as a farm wife. Suppose, like Hennie, he doesn't approve of his wife wearing pants?

Mr. Booysen

Lucy assured me there would be no problem with Mr. Booysen (pronounced BOY-sen) but I was skeptical. I described the reaction I had gotten in Middelpoort from school authorities who refused to let me visit. "He's likely to be suspicious of me," I warned her. "Administrators in Afrikaner schools don't like Americans, and he'll decide I'm another journalist trying to make South Africa look bad."

"Nonsense," she said. "I know Mr. Booysen personally. He's not at all like that. I've left a message for him, and the secretary will call us right back."

The phone rang. I listened to this side of the conversation in Afrikaans. I didn't understand the words, but I understood the tone. Lucy hung up, looking apologetic. "Mr. Booysen sends word that it's impossible for you to come and visit. Exams are being written, and the children have to study every minute. And the inspectors are there, so naturally he can't have an outsider around."

I blew up. "'No' is the wrong answer," I said, turning into an aggressive American. "I'm going anyway."

Lucy was shocked, but Hennie took my side. "I agree. Go anyway."

"We'll simply go and pay a visit to Kristin," I said.

"But we can't," Lucy protested. "Not if she's having exams."

"We won't stay long. Half an hour. And you're her mother. You have a right to stop in and see your daughter for half an hour if you want to, don't you? And anyway I don't believe there are exams or inspectors. I think it's a . . . fabrication."

"You don't think he's lying!"

"I do."

"Go," said Hennie.

Lucy and I drove into Reedsville, three-quarters of an hour from the farm, past drought-parched fields blackened and smoky with veld fires. We did not go directly to the school; we went instead to Mr. Booysen's house. The headmaster was not at home. We went down the street and had a cup of tea with Lucy's aunt. I watched the time slip away. It was almost five o'clock when we went back to Mr. Booysen's.

"Not everyone likes him," Lucy said. "Many people consider him rude, but he's done a good job with the school. I think his rudeness is really just *directness*."

He came out to meet us in tennis shorts, a handsome, stocky, silver-haired man. He lives on the main street in a modern house with a book-lined living room, plush-covered Victorian chairs and ornate tables arranged around the walls like a doctor's waiting room.

I thought his rudeness was really just rudeness. Mr. Booysen wasted no time in launching his attack on America and Americans while his thin, long-faced wife served us yet another cup of tea.

"The whole world is against us," he complained, a line I heard over and over. "They've been against us for three hundred years. They have no idea what it's like, and yet they try to tell us how to run our country. As though you have been so kind to your Blacks! As though you don't have apartheid in your country! And your journalists! All they show on American television is violence, violence. Everyone thinks this country is on fire. Have *you* seen any violence?"

It was after five o'clock. I was not interested in an argument or even a debate. I wanted to see the school, and my patience was worn through.

"Mr. Booysen," I said. "I'm here to write a book for teenagers. I'm not a CIA agent or a communist agitator or a journalist looking for sensation. Either you believe that I am who I say I am, and that I'm doing what I say I'm doing and we get on with it, or you don't believe me and I leave."

"Go see the school," he said, standing up to escort us to the door.

Kristin Potgieter

It was dinnertime when we pulled up in front of the hostel. Boys and girls stood in separate lines outside the dining hall, ready to file in. The bell had already rung, but the arrival of two adults stopped them; they waited respectfully until we had passed. Then at a signal they marched in and took places at tables for ten, boys and girls at each table, a senior student assigned to help the younger ones. The girls sat down and the boys remained standing while someone said grace, both before and after the meal.

Kristin rushed out to greet Lucy with a hug and a kiss. She is a pretty, rosy-cheeked girl in jeans, a yellow sweater, and tackies, South African for sneakers. Lucy recently went on a shopping trip to Durban, several hours' drive from Reedsville, to buy Kristin some clothes. But she was appalled by the big shirts, baggy skirts, and brilliant clashing colors that were in fashion, and instead came back with conservative jeans and sweaters.

Kristin offered to skip dinner to take us to the hostel. Unlike her frilly, girlish room at home, her room in the hostel is spartan. Kristin has it to herself because she is a prefect, elected to this honor by the other students. She wonders how much of an honor it is to be responsible for helping with the younger children.

Her uniforms hang neatly in a wardrobe: navy blue jumpers with white shirts and striped ties. In cold weather they wear pants instead of skirts, and in summer they switch to light blue cotton jumpers. The floors shine with fresh wax. At one end is the study hall, where all the girls on the floor go to do their homework. At the other end is the room occupied by one of the teachers who serves as housemother, exchanging privacy for cheap rent. There are six teachers and eighty students in the school, most of them children from surrounding farms and all but a few boarding in the hostel. Boys and girls live in wings of the same building, separated by a dining hall and a common room.

Kristin and Lucy discussed Jeannette, Kristin's seven-year-old cousin who is much indulged by her mother, Lucy's sister-in-law. "Jeannette refuses to leave her mother and stay in the hostel with the other children, and so Elise drives all the way in from the farm each morning, drops the little girl off at school, and stays with *her* mother until it's time to pick Jeannette up again," she said disapprovingly. "Elise should ignore the tears and insist that Jeannette stay in the hostel with the other children."

The separation is difficult, Lucy admits. "I remember how Kristin cried and carried on when she first went to the hostel, but I was very firm about it," Lucy said. "I also remember when I was seven and packed off to the hostel without knowing a word of Afrikaans. I spoke only Xhosa, which is what my nanny spoke. She had to stay with me until I began to learn the language of the other children." Jeannette speaks Afrikaans, however, and Elise doesn't have that as an excuse.

Downstairs in the dining hall dinner had ended and the final thanksgiving was pronounced. The students were free to indulge in half an hour of television, the maximum daily allowance, before they were due at their monitored study halls for the evening's work. Kristin lured a couple of girl-friends away from the television to meet me, and for ten minutes or so we stood awkwardly in the middle of the dining room and attempted to talk about their plans for the future. One girl wants to go to the University of Pretoria to study fashion design; another is thinking of the University of Cape Town for biology. Kristin, like her brothers, is slated for Stellenbosch.

Totally unsatisfactory.

"Mr. Booysen said the message he got from his secretary was that you wanted to address the student body," Lucy told me as we left the hostel. "Naturally that was impossible."

"Naturally."

What I had asked for was an opportunity to meet two or three students and maybe sit in on a couple of classes, although I would not have understood the language. Mr. Booysen had had his way and outmaneuvered the bloody American after all, and Lucy Potgieter is a nice lady who would never dream of breaking the rules.

The Bull Sale

I asked Lucy to take me to the farm school on her father-in-law's property, but by now she was weary of the subject. It would require written application, she said, and that would have to be put through the local educational machinery to obtain approval, a process that would take a week or so. Obviously I did not have time. I remembered the ease with which I had visited Koos van der Merwe's farm school in Middelpoort and doubted the excuses. The defensiveness, the paranoia were everywhere.

106

"The woman who teaches on my father-in-law's farm school is paid far more than she deserves," Lucy huffed. "She's been there for years. She teaches only a few hours a day. I doubt that they learn much from her. But the government pays her a good salary for that. The thing is, though," she added, "you're making me think about things I never have before. I never questioned that the schools for Blacks are different."

"Forget the school," Hennie said. "We're going to a bull sale."

The major farmers of the Reedsville area gathered on a cold, blustery morning on Etienne Malan's farm to bid on 350 of his young steers and heifers and 60 prize bulls. Lucy dressed up for this occasion, and Hennie donned his old commando jacket and battered bush hat. It was nearly an hour's drive over dirt roads, but we were to be there by nine o'clock. Hennie parked the Mercedes in a line of Mercedeses, apparently the official Boer automobile. About fifty Afrikaners, farmers and their wives, gathered inside a brick house as big as a motel around a lace-covered table for morning tea. The table was spread with cakes of all sorts and platters of *koeksisters*: twists of dough, deep-fried and drenched in honey syrup. They could become addictive.

South Africans like their tea strong with milk and lots of sugar. When I first arrived in South Africa I asked for my preference, "tea with lemon," which they translated as "lemon tea" and treated as an oddity. Assuming that all Americans are coffee drinkers, some people served me coffee even though I don't like it. "But you're an American!" they would say. "All Americans drink coffee!" In Middelpoort the van der Merwes went out of their way to put orange juice on the already overloaded breakfast table because they understood that Americans must have their orange juice. And in Stellenbosch the professor's wife set a pitcher of ice water in front of me; I was the only one with a water glass. They don't drink water with their meals, but they are sure that Americans do. By the time I reached Reedsville I was drinking tea strong, sweet, and milky, like everyone else.

With starvation again at bay (we had eaten the usual enormous farm breakfast only an hour or so earlier), we went outside to listen to a local expert describe the fine points of one of Malan's prize bulls. Then everyone gathered under a tree where a side of beef swung from a limb and watched a butcher demonstrate the best way to turn a side of beef into a pile of steaks and roasts. The farmers laughed and joked among themselves, a hardy-looking lot, all in commando jackets and bush hats. A few wore shorts and knee socks, despite the temperature, their knees glowing red from the cold. Most of the women had retreated into the house, hugging their arms.

Just before noon everyone gathered on the stoep for "light refreshments," champagne and little sandwiches. Lucy said it was against the law to serve liquor before a stock sale, but apparently a glass or two of champagne did not count. Thus fortified, everyone trooped down to a shed with rows of bleacher seats around a show ring, the auctioneer mounted a podium, and Malan, a burly man in a brown fedora, signaled to his Black helpers to release the first lot. Ten animals jammed the ring, and the bidding began. It was in English —the auctioneer was English-speaking, though no one else there was—and in a few seconds the first lot had been knocked down to a buyer and was chased out as the second lot stomped and bawled in the chute.

Bidders were casual, if not downright secretive. Most of the yearlings were going to a man who never interrupted his conversation with the farmer next to him, wiggling one finger of the hand cupped under his chin to indicate a bid. The sun had vanished, and a chill wind blasted us. Huddled in jackets and sweaters borrowed from Mrs. Malan, hands stuffed in pockets and the feeling long gone from our feet, we sat through thirty-five lots, waiting for the main event—the sale of thirty bulls bred from a line imported from Germany and thirty Afrikaner crossbreeds. One by one the huge, powerful animals lumbered into the ring. Bids climbed to five times what the yearlings were bringing.

"Sold to Mr. Hennie Potgieter!" the auctioneer announced.

"I think you just bought a bull," I said to Lucy.

She nodded sadly. "There goes the new kitchen."

Mrs. Malan and her friends bustled in and out of the kitchen where several Black maids had been working all morning. Black farm workers set up outdoor grills in preparation for the *braaivleis* (BRY-flays), the South African equivalent of a barbecue.

Soon smoke was curling from the fires, and the meat began to sizzle: *boerewors*, bursting their skins; *sosatie*, chunks of lamb marinated in curry and threaded on wooden skewers with onion and dried apricot; lamb ribs basted with spicy sauce; fat lamb chops, dripping juice.

We began politely enough with plates, napkins, and silverware, but these were set aside and we grabbed the meat in our hands as it came off the grills, pausing now and then to help ourselves from bowls of *vetkoeks*, "fatcakes," little fried breads stuffed with honey, cinnamon, and butter. Lamb bones began to pile up on the ground. I was on my fourth *sosatie* and had lost count of *vetkoeks* when Lucy said, "Save room for pudding."

"Pudding" in South Africa means dessert of all kinds. The salads had been cleared from the long table on the stoep and replaced with cakes, cookies, ice cream, and an elegant trifle concocted of rum-soaked cake, raspberry jam, and custard arranged in layers, heaped with whipped cream. That was the one English contribution to the meal.

109

When we had eaten we again separated according to sex, customary among the Afrikaners. The women retired inside and sat sipping more tea. The men stayed outside, red-nosed and red-kneed, proving their hardihood. Some of the women brought out their knitting and crocheting. The conversation, conducted in English out of courtesy to me, focused on food, diets, children, fashion, and pregnancy. At least it was not about politics.

I looked longingly out the window at the Boers in their commando jackets, swigging Coca-Cola, which seemed to me a strange drink for such a chilly day. They seemed to be having a good time, talking, I supposed, about bulls and other such male subjects in Afrikaans. It would have been improper for me to go out and join them. I tried to pay attention to the women. One had an elaborately braided hairstyle. "Who did it for you?" someone asked. "My girls," she said. "I always have my girls do my hair." She was referring to her Black maids, calling them girls regardless of age, as White men often call Black men "boys."

At the end of the long afternoon, the men began to pop into the house just long enough to claim their wives, who hastily packed away their yarn and needles, thanked the hostess, and scurried after their husbands. Eventually Hennie came for Lucy and me. That was when I realized that the farmers were drinking something more than plain Coca-Cola. "Cane and coke," Hennie explained—cane spirits, distilled from sugar cane, used to spike the soft drink.

We were halfway home when we came upon the accident. As we topped the rise on the tarred road, we saw a car stopped on the roadway and a White man standing near it. "Somebody killed a Kaffir," Hennie said, and for a moment I misunderstood and thought he had said somebody killed a *calf*. But as we drew closer, I saw the body on the road, the Black man's face bloody and his eyes blank and staring.

110

The groceries he had been carrying lay scattered on the road. Hennie stopped to help the White man who had been driving the car, its windshield smashed and hood dented, but the police were already on the way.

"Probably drunk," Hennie said as we drove off. "Stupid Kaffirs. Drunk all the time. Hit the hooter and they step out right in front of you, and then there's a hell of a mess."

When we got back to the farm, Hennie built a fire in the fireplace and we settled down to review the events of the day, kept company by the housedog, a miniature dachshund named Snoopy. (Outside a large black dog with a menacing growl protects the place, giving Lucy a sense of security when Hennie is away and effectively discouraging me as well from doing much prowling around the grounds. Hennie would like her to keep a gun handy, as most Whites do, but Lucy is afraid of guns.)

Now I learned about Snoopy and clocks. An old clock hangs on the wall behind the sofa opposite the one on which Lucy sat, Snoopy's head on her lap. Alerted by the small whirring sound made by the clock seconds before it began to strike the hour, Snoopy awoke from his snooze with a start, raced across the room, leaped up on the sofa back, and barked fiercely at the striking clock. The clock finished its seven bongs and Snoopy, satisfied that he had vanquished the monster, trotted proudly back to Lucy's lap. He dozed peacefully for fifty-nine minutes and fifty-eight seconds, until the clock whirred again and Snoopy charged into battle. This time it took him *eight* bongs to bark it into submission. Apparently this goes on twenty-four hours a day, as long as Snoopy is within range of the clock.

While waiting for the hour to pass and the silly dachshund to attack again, we gossiped. I asked about a young woman in an eye-dazzling red-and-white-striped jumpsuit and too much makeup who had been going on at great length about

111

starting a dancing school in Reedsville. She had once been a dancing teacher in Johannesburg, and she was certain that the young people of Reedsville would benefit from learning some of the traditional dances, like the waltz and the tango. Lucy suggested that Hennie might also benefit from such instruction, a suggestion made in jest but greeted with an unmistakable harrumph. The dancer is on her third husband, Lucy said, describing one of the middle-aged men in knee socks and short pants. Lucy is much opposed to divorce.

"Tell her about du Toit," Hennie said.

"You tell her," Lucy said.

"Du Toit is color-blind," Hennie told me. I must have looked totally blank. "He doesn't know Black from White," he explained. "That's why his wife left him."

I still did not get it.

Hennie made another attempt to overcome my dullness. "He buggered around with his servants."

Finally I caught on. The English use the vulgar phrase "bugger around with" to mean "have sexual relations with." Apparently du Toit, whoever he was, had had sexual relations with his Black maids. Until only a couple of weeks before my visit to Reedsville, sexual relations between people of different races were strictly prohibited by law and punished by years in prison. Interracial marriages were forbidden as well under another law, the Prohibition of Mixed Marriages Act of 1949.

"It's wrong, what he did," Lucy said.

"It's because niggers are not like us," Hennie said. "They're not as far up the evolutionary scale as Whites are, they're more like animals. It's immoral and disgusting to have sex with an animal, and it's immoral and disgusting for a White man to have sex with a Black woman."

"They're like children," Lucy said, softening it a little. "It's taking advantage of the master-servant relationship. My brother is a lawyer in Bloemfontein, and he says the reason for enacting the Immorality Act was to prevent farmers from taking advantage of their Black help."

I was relieved when the clock whirred and the dog leaped to action. He vanquished it after an exhausting ten strokes.

VII

PIETERMARITZBURG

◢◢◢◢◢ **N**amed after a couple of doughty Voortrekkers, Piet Retief and Gert Maritz, Pietermaritzburg is an unlikely name for a city where the Union Jack still flies over the Victoria Club. Locals shorten it to "Maritzburg" or even "PMB." It is a thoroughly English-feeling town, the capital of Natal, the most thoroughly English-feeling of the South African provinces. PMB's population of barely 200,000 divides roughly into thirds of White, Black, and Asian, with a small contingent of Coloureds.

The first recorded footfall of an Englishman in Natal occurred in 1699 when an ironically named ship, *Fidelity*, put three crewmen ashore to trade for ivory but never came back to pick them up. Over a century later the 1820 settlers arrived in the eastern Cape; soon after, the English began to settle in Natal as well. Some Cape merchants decided to begin trading in Port Natal, which they renamed Durban in 1835 in honor of Sir Benjamin d'Urban, governor of the Cape Colony.

For the next few years there was unease in this frontier area. To keep the peace between Voortrekkers and Zulus, the Cape government sent an occupation force to Durban. When the English soldiers were withdrawn in 1839, the trekkers established the Republic of Natalia with the capital at Pietermaritzburg. This on-again-off-again situation, the British operating out of Durban and the Boers out of Maritzburg, lasted four years. Finally the British annexed the republic in 1844, changing the name back to Natal. Most of the Voortrekkers left.

Without them there were few Whites left in the area, and the economy went downhill fast. Schemes to bring in groups of settlers usually failed. A few German families arrived with the intention of growing cotton, but that did not work; some stayed anyway and tried other kinds of farming. Then a British opportunist named Joseph Byrne promoted a real estate and immigration scheme that would have made him rich if it had succeeded; between 1849 and 1851 he brought in over three thousand English people and settled them on poor land with little water. Byrne went bankrupt, but most of his settlers hung on somehow. From then on immigration to southern Africa was steady but slow, never equal to the numbers of people who headed for the United States and Canada to begin new lives.

It was not the struggling immigrants who made Natal "the last outpost of the British Empire," but the men of the Forty-fifth Regiment. Without much soldiering required of them, the English soldiers passed the time playing cricket and putting on dramas. Soon a society was established to promote the arts in Durban. Meanwhile Queen Victoria, who had ascended the English throne in 1837, was having a deep effect on the manners and morals of her subjects. Her influence was felt and absorbed even in the most distant of her colonies. Some say it has never been lost in Natal, handed down from generation to generation.

Lisa and Colin O'Neill

Only a few hours drive from Reedsville where morning frosts nipped away new growth, it was spring in Pietermaritzburg. The trees were green, avocados and mulberries ripe in the O'Neills' garden. Flowers bloomed under the watchful eyes of a rooster named Ralph whose crow ends in a strangled squawk, a strutting bantam, an elderly cat, a smallish dog named Percy, and Heinz, a very large Doberman. They all belong to Colin O'Neill, age thirteen, who fancies animals.

Terrence and Elizabeth O'Neill had gone out for the evening, and Lisa, sixteen, volunteered to fix supper for Colin and me. Lisa was beginning a forty-hour fast to benefit the starving people of Africa, especially the Ethiopians, and this would be her last meal until Sunday noon. She had collected pledges from family and friends, an average of ten cents an hour, with the exception of a "Mr. C. M. O'Neill," entered in her book at a penny an hour for a grand total of forty cents. Mr. C. M. O'Neill turned out to be Colin. (South Africans prefer to use initials rather than full names. Newspaper articles, for example, always refer to "President P. W. Botha," not "Pieter Botha.")

Lisa scrambled eggs with cheese, fixed a big salad with avocados from the tree in the garden, and mixed mulberries and her mother's homemade yogurt for dessert. Colin, in the absence of his mother, feasted on his favorite meal of chips with tomato sauce. I told him that in America the combination is known as french fries with ketchup and that American mothers do not favor this diet any more than South African mothers do.

116

"*French* fries? Why are they called french fries?"

"I don't know."

"Why do you call tomato sauce *ketchup*?"

I didn't know how to account for this cultural difference either.

In honor of Lisa's fast Colin repeated a number of ghastly Ethiopian jokes until Lisa made him stop.

Lisa is a tall, thin girl, quiet and intense, who hopes to become a journalist and may go to the University of Natal, which has campuses in Pietermaritzburg and Durban. Colin has a few years to make up his mind what he wants, but right now he dreams of a way to combine his two main loves, sport and money. (In South Africa one is involved in "sport," not "sports.") He loves animals; maybe he'll have a farm. He likes fly fishing and wears an Orvis patch on his jacket, the label of an American manufacturer of fishing equipment. He is also crazy about boardsailing, a blend of surfing and sailing (called windsurfing in the United States). Maybe, he speculated, he could be a businessman dealing in sporting equipment. That got him onto the subject of hunting; he likes to shoot birds with his father.

One romantic possibility is to become a ranger in one of the nine national parks in South Africa or dozens of private game reserves, some belonging to the provinces, some privately owned. Kruger National Park is the largest and best known. Tourists from all over the world come to see elephant, giraffe, hippo, rhino, zebra, lion, leopard, and twenty-nine species of antelope.

"Are you worried about the future?" I asked them.

Colin shrugged. "I'll go live in the bush if it comes to that." By "that" we both understood the collapse of White dominance and a bloody takeover by Blacks.

But Lisa voiced concern. "I feel so helpless," she said. "There seems to be no way to change anything. We're not allowed to discuss political problems at school. Among the

117

racialists there's nothing to discuss anyway." (South Africans use the term "racialist," a British word, rather than the American "racist.") "They don't see any particular problem, and if they won't admit there's a problem, there's no way you can convince them things have to change."

Except for a maid who comes by bus from the township each day to do housework, Lisa and Colin are not acquainted with any Blacks and know little about them, but in spite of this they are sympathetic. In primary school they both studied units on African tribes, but when I described the initiation school in Middelpoort, they were amazed; they had never heard of this.

Colin was currently studying Switzerland at school, but he is much more interested in the United States. Some of what he knows he has learned in school, but most of it he picked up from movies and television programs, like *Hill Street Blues.* Two American movies making the rounds of South African cinemas at that time were *Rambo* and *Desperately Seeking Susan.* I cringed to think of the picture of my country he has put together from these sources. Colin confessed that he likes the "really horrific" horror movies. The film industry in South Africa is quite small, although one export has made a big hit in the United States: *The Gods Must Be Crazy,* by director Jamie Uys, the story of a Bushman (Khoisan) from the Kalahari Desert in western South Africa. Uys (pronounced ACE) is said to be working on a follow-up to that film.

If there is one thing Colin envies about Americans, it is their wide choice of TV, available virtually around the clock from several networks, cable, movie channels, and so on. South Africa has had television only since 1975, one channel which gives equal time to English and Afrikaans programs. It goes on the air at 5:30 P.M. on weekdays, 2:30 on Saturdays, and 4:30 on Sundays. About 60 percent of the programs are

118

produced in South Africa, and the rest are imports, many from America. Two other channels broadcast Black programming in Zulu, Xhosa, Tswana, and Sotho. Television is tightly controlled by the government; read that as "censored." For example, no scenes of violence in the Black townships may be shown on TV; as a result, many South Africans have seen far less of what is happening in their country than we have. Nevertheless, many hardliners believe that even this control is too light-handed and blame many of South Africa's problems directly or indirectly on the influence of television.

"Tell us about Harlem," Colin invited me. "Have you ever been there?"

I said I had, but I didn't really know much about it.

"Is it true that there's a big sign at the gate that says 'Enter at your own risk'?"

To the best of my knowledge there is no gate and no sign. I admitted that the reason I don't know much about Harlem is because I don't feel comfortable being a minority White in a Black area—and that gives me some insight into how it must feel to be a White South African.

Lisa is one of the eight school reporters on the "editorial team" of *Schools Witness*, a monthly supplement to the Pietermaritzburg newspaper. Eight high schools are represented. The lead story, headlined "Try a bit of flair," is about two "matrics" who earn extra pocket money by making and decorating clothes; one designs and sews, one uses an airbrush to decorate plain white shirts. What makes this front page news is that they are *boys*—and one of them plays rugby.

"Tops of the Pops" listed the Top Ten in South Africa that month. "We Are the World" headed the list, with hits by Bruce Springsteen (a special favorite of Lisa's), Duran Duran, and Power Station, as well as musicians from the U.K. (the United Kingdom, as Great Britain is usually called). A review

of new releases criticized the album titled *We Are the World*
with ten previously unreleased songs. "Disappointing,"
warned the reviewer, "not worth the album price. Unless
you're an American music devotee don't be conned by the
big names." But most of them *are* devotees of American music. South Africa has no bands or singers to brag about,
according to Colin.

A new hangout called "Shapes" had opened for the "under
seventeens" on Wednesday and Friday nights, and a reporter
went to check it out.

> They flock to Pietermaritzburg's only suitable night-
> club in their overdressed droves for a rave on the town
> [she wrote]. Teenagers donned earrings, spikes, make-
> up and duffel coats and hit the old renovated church
> hall. Being alcohol-free, it is obviously popular among
> parents who now have no excuse to keep their kids
> at home!
>
> On entering, the sudden impact of three black walls
> is lifted by the glowing, fluorescent shapes on the
> fourth. Sweeping white lights illuminate the mixed
> expressions on the faces of the revellers. . . . While
> elbowing one's neighbour, one also becomes increas-
> ingly aware of the inevitable pall of cigarette smoke
> which swirls thickly. . . . Full marks for the sound
> system. Speakers thump out the beat above the heads
> of the dancers and an ultraviolet light causes teeth to
> glow weirdly in the smokey gloom.

There was an article about courses in teen self-awareness,
a plea from a girl who believes her school should be run by
a parliamentary system of elected representatives, and a story
about a French horn player, the only PMB school repre-
sentative in the National Youth Orchestra. The usual stuff.

But there was also this article by a student from a Black

high school: "This is being written at a time when it should be clear to us young people, regardless of colour, that the future is up to us to mould it the way we want it to be." He described an unusual event in South Africa, a multiracial gathering of top scholars from various racial groups in Pietermaritzburg. "It was somewhat incredible to me to see blacks and whites, sitting together, sharing ideas, while having their delicious supper. . . . I was happy to discover that many a white pupil is willing to have this country governed on a non-racial basis."

Such get-togethers tend to be rare and one-sided. "Our choir also visited Collegiate for a lunchtime concert and were received with appreciation. . . . I have wondered why white schools never visit black schools, but Maritzburg College charmed my heart by letting their chess team come and face our newly formed chess team. . . . I feel somehow obliged to thank these two schools which dared having fun with us. I know it is not easy as we are 15 kilometres from town and some of those are along a bad road, but I appeal to other schools to befriend themselves with other races, so as to stimulate a better relationship among races."

In that article, Blacks trying to learn about Whites; in another interesting piece, English trying to learn about Afrikaners. An English-speaking girl named Sarah decided to attend an Afrikaans high school. Tired of bad marks in her poorest subject, Sarah, a Standard Eight pupil [tenth grade] at an English-medium school, arranged to spend six weeks at Voortrekker Hoerskool.

Her aim was to improve her Afrikaans, but she wound up learning about a different culture and a different school system. She admitted that she took her biases to Voortrekker with her but lost most of them along the way.

Sarah discovered that the Afrikaans culture has a strong influence on the school. At English-speaking schools, discipline is upheld mostly by the prefect body [student leaders], whereas at Voortrekker the prefects are more like figureheads and it is the teachers who do the disciplining.

'There is great respect for the teachers,' said Sarah. In the classroom situation pupils are not encouraged to give their opinion or speak unless they are asked to.

Sarah feels that Afrikaners are more prepared to speak English than the English are to speak Afrikaans. She says this may be because English is recognized as the world's first language, whereas Afrikaans is only a South African language. She feels that more English people should make an effort to speak Afrikaans.

In each issue *Schools Witness* runs a letter-writing competition on a controversial topic and publishes a dozen or so of the best letters. That issue dealt with the subject of sport, and the students were vehement in their responses. The first-prize letter, which won the writer a 35-millimeter camera, went like this: "Sport in schools! Sometimes I wonder whether 'schools in sport' might not be a more apt description. But in a sport-mad country like our own, where the aforementioned activity frequently takes pride of place above both local and world disasters on official news broadcasts, what can you expect?" But someone on the other side snorted, "The argument that sport fosters exclusivity is absolute balderdash . . . schools should keep sport in their plans for the future. Defeat brings experience and knowledge while winning serves to blacken out already dull parts of life."

A student worried about the neurotic emphasis placed on competition wrote, "The sport which comes to mind immediately is rugby which tends to attract the 'macho men' in the school. These rugby players ridicule other sports as inferior and 'naffish,' and those intellectuals not competing in any sport are scorned and picked on. . . . The more academic sports such as chess are ridiculed and are taken part in only by the real 'nerds.'"

Another letter: "In South African schools the honour to wear a first team rugby jersey seems to be the alpha and omega of school life. Many girls and boys are excluded from peer groups because their sporting ability seems to be less prominent than those of others." Nevertheless, "It would be absurd, sir, to suggest that sport should be stopped in schools."

"Those who show skill in sport, regardless of other academic abilities, are considered prime examples of what a good citizen should be like," someone wrote. "Those who do not play well are proven to be unworthy of being a 'real' man!" The writer, noting that he had spent many of his schooldays outside of the country, commented "I see this as one of the many deplorable aspects of South African schools" and ended "I am more than ever inclined to spend my time away from Kipling's 'flannelled fools at the wicket and muddied oafs at the goals.'"

"Flanneled fools at the wicket" refers to cricket, a bat and ball game introduced by the British. The bowler hurls the hard, leather-covered ball at a wicket, attempting to knock down one of the cross-pieces. The wicket is defended by a batsman. Lisa says it's boring to watch. Colin, who demonstrated the graceful, straight-armed bowl, says it's "a gentleman's game." It is, in any case, a forerunner of baseball.

"Muddied oafs at the goal" are rugby players. Rugby, also of English origin, is similar to football but with no time-outs or substitutions. It is especially an Afrikaner obsession. The South African professional team is called the Springboks, named for a kind of antelope.

*   *   *

Newsweek arrived in the O'Neills' mailbox with a cover story headlined, "SOUTH AFRICA: WHAT CAN BE DONE?" The photograph was an extreme close-up of a Black man, a single tear rolling down his cheek.

"This issue has been banned," Terrence said. "We were lucky to get our copy."

Later I read that an article titled "The Young Lions," about angry young Blacks, had prompted the government to expel the reporter from the country. Now the September 16 issue of an American newsmagazine had become a collector's item.

The Birthday Party

The spring weather had turned cold and rainy, and Elizabeth O'Neill was worried. Sunday was Terrence's fiftieth birthday, and fifty people were invited for lunch to celebrate. Elizabeth preferred to entertain them on the terrace by the swimming pool, rather than have them all jammed into the house.

Saturday was the day to get ready for the party. First thing Saturday morning Lisa, still on her fast, had to be driven to her public high school on the other side of town to play basketball for Pell House. There are about a thousand girls in the high school, and the girls are assigned to "houses" of a hundred each. Lisa and her older sister, Anne, a matric student, are both in Pell House. Anne has gone to "Durbs" (Durban) until Sunday and is not around to help either.

I volunteered. The menu featured chicken in a curry-tomato sauce, a dish served at an event honoring Queen Elizabeth II of England. Half a dozen chickens have been cooking and cooling, a few at a time, since early morning, and my job was to skin and bone the birds and cut up the meat. While I was up to my elbows in chicken, various people came and went. Cleo, the maid, brought her sister, Regina, to work. Cleo sat on the kitchen floor, polishing the silver. Elizabeth hastened to assure me that Cleo *always* sits on the floor and that she will not ever accept an invitation to sit on a chair in the lounge or anywhere else. Later Colin brought a friend to meet the woman who lives in the land of unlimited television; the boy's name is Tony, but Colin introduced him as "Weasel."

Next Elizabeth's friend Clare drove up with four more chickens for me to deal with and introduced an innovative way of cooking a vast quantity of rice: by sealing it in a styrofoam picnic basket with boiling water. None of us had much faith that this would really work, and as a matter of fact it did not. We stopped for lunch (not chicken, thank goodness—Clare brought a quiche) and Elizabeth got Clare to tell me the story of her maid, with the unlikely name of Adorable.

The maid had worked for Clare for thirteen years, long enough to know each other well. Adorable was the mother of eight children; Clare has none. One Saturday Clare thought Adorable looked unwell and offered to drive her to the bus stop; Adorable declined. An hour went by, and it became apparent to Clare that Adorable was definitely ill. The maid refused Clare's offer to take her to a hospital. She did say, though, that she would like to go home early, and she went into the bathroom to wash up. Time passed. Clare knocked on the bathroom door and asked if she was all right. The maid called out that she was. Eventually the door opened and Adorable emerged, carrying a newborn baby, her ninth. Adorable had not wanted to bother Mrs. Clare with her personal problem, and Clare had not even been aware that her maid of thirteen years had "fallen pregnant."

"Ag, shame!" Elizabeth said, a typical South African exclamation, even though she knew Clare's story well.

All of us were up early the sunny morning of Terrence's

125

fiftieth birthday, presenting him with his gifts before he was even out of bed. As sometimes happened when I dropped into people's lives for even a short time, I had made an intimate connection with this family, sleeping in Anne's bed while she was in Durban, moving the notebooks off her desk to make room for mine, shunting her school uniforms to one side of the closet to hang up my clothes, and greeting her father with a birthday hug before he had a chance to shave or dress.

Breakfast was lighter in this English household. Lisa was still on her fast for the starving Ethiopians and had only a small glass of juice. Terrence ate a couple of eggs, Colin poured a bowl of cold cereal, and Elizabeth and I had toast and anchovette—anchovy paste. I also tried spreading my toast with Bovril, the thick, salty base for making beef broth. An acquired taste, I thought, like the creamed tripe and onions served the night before. That was my first experience with this traditional English dish, the rubbery lining of a cow's stomach that loses some (but not all) of its rubberiness with long cooking.

After breakfast Terrence and Colin were dispatched to the grocery store for last-minute items for the party. Terrence carefully wheeled his 1958 Jaguar out of the garage for its weekly outing; in mint condition, it is his cherished indulgence, lovingly restored, the seats upholstered in soft leather, the walnut instrument panel well polished. I went along for the ride.

We wound through the beautiful suburbs of Pietermaritzburg and up to a vantage point overlooking the city. Voortrekkers had once stood here and looked east, toward Durban and the Indian Ocean forty miles away. In the center of the panorama lay the heart of the city and its expensive White residential areas. To the north were little pockets of land, a fraction of the size of the White area, set aside for Indians

126

and for Coloureds. Far to the south was a long, crescent-shaped valley crowded with poor Black townships.

At home the champagne was on ice, someone had brought platters of smoked trout, and Elizabeth was fussing over the cooler full of half-cooked rice.

The guests began to arrive at noon, three dozen adults, all couples, and a dozen or so teenagers. The adults crowded into the family room near the bar and the young people sat outside on the terrace sipping fruit juice. At one o'clock champagne was passed around, and everyone gathered for the toast. We held our glasses until the bubbles went flat, listening to a long speech about our good friend Terrence. Terrence responded with a salute to his wife, his children, his old friends. Then he turned and raised his glass to "my newest friend, all the way from America." Enough to give anyone a lump in the throat.

There are common stereotypes in South Africa, easy traps for the unwary visitor. One goes that the Afrikaners are hard-nosed, stubborn, anti-Black, and unwilling to give up their privileges of wealth and power, while the English are open-minded, Black-loving, and liberal. This stereotype is contra-dicted by another that says the Afrikaners may be tough and stubborn, but they are honest and open and genuinely caring in their relationships with the Blacks who work for them and who know exactly where they stand with them, while the English are hypocritical, talk a liberal line, but do nothing to help Blacks. What I observed was a spectrum: some English are quite liberal, some Afrikaners are hopelessly conserva-tive, but there are a lot of other stances in between.

Margaret Glass was a surprise. She jumped all over me in the first fifteen minutes of the party, apparently holding me personally responsible for South Africa's bad reputation in the world's press and particularly in American media. "You people just don't know what it's like," she insisted—a refrain

I heard repeatedly from Afrikaners, but Margaret had emigrated years before from the United Kingdom to marry a South African. I edged away from her. Then my hostess caught me and led me off to meet "that rare breed, a liberal Afrikaner."

Sam Cloete *is* something of a rare breed. A teacher for years in an Afrikaans-medium school, he had decided that he needed to find more meaning in his life, quit that job, and was now the head of a technical college for Blacks. He backed me into Terrence's empty study and insisted that I had to change my plans—either stay in Pietermaritzburg a few more days and visit his school or delay going on to Johannesburg and come back to Pietermaritzburg from Durban, where I was going in an hour. As an added incentive, he promised to arrange an escorted trip to KwaZulu, one of the Black homelands. "You cannot write a book about this country without visiting KwaZulu," he insisted.

It was an argument I heard at every stop—that I was moving too fast, missing too much, not getting an accurate picture, going home with skewed ideas. A few more days here, a stop there, that would make things right. I knew there was truth in the argument. Obviously I could learn more in three months than I could in five weeks; but I did not *have* three months. A trip to Sam's technical college and on to KwaZulu would have been wonderful, but I would have had to cut out something else—either time I needed in Johannesburg or my longed-for visit to a game reserve, three days in the bush where the only black-and-white situation I would have to think about was a herd of zebra, and if I were lucky, some rhino. I took Sam's business card, promising that I would try but knowing I would not, and went to look for Lisa and her friends.

Before it started to rain we sat on the terrace and listened to Anne tell about her trip to Durbs. She stayed in a flat belonging to a friend's sister, and they went to a nightclub and danced to disco music and drank. The legal drinking age in South Africa is eighteen, but Anne and her seventeen-year-old friends all pretend to be old enough. The club charges a general admission, five rands for girls, ten rands for boys, and the drinks are free.

The weekend had been to recuperate from writing her "trials," practice exams for the matrics. The trials had exhausted her, each running three hours, much longer than the exams she is accustomed to. Except for science and maths (South Africans say "maths" instead of "math"), all the exams were essay questions. The matrics, held in November, all last for three hours each. Anne has no idea what she wants to do after matric, a situation that vaguely bothers her but worries her parents much more. Like many English-speaking parents, Terrence and Elizabeth want their children to have a good education in a solid profession so they will be able to leave the country "when the crunch comes."

Not *if*. *When*. Terrence and Elizabeth intend to stay where they are. "We are South Africans," they told me one evening. "This is our home and we'll stick it out no matter what happens. But we want our children to have the option." Another cherished stereotype is that English speakers do not have the love of land and country that Afrikaners do. Sometimes for their own sake or the sake of their children, they leave—or prepare their children to leave. A local joke is the definition of a patriot: "A man who can't sell his house." Afrikaners do not speak of leaving.

The night before the party we sat in the lounge and told stories about our lives. Terrence and Elizabeth are both products of "mixed marriages." Terrence's ancestors came out from Ireland generations ago. Each O'Neill generation married Afrikaner women but continued to practice Catholicism. "When my father died a few years ago," Terrence said, "the

129

priest stood outside drinking whiskey with the men, while the *predikant* sat inside with the women drinking tea."

Elizabeth's father was Afrikaner, her mother English. "Since we both grew up in a mixture, we're a good mix ourselves. We understand both sides, and we share the same value system. When we were married, our first big decision was to 'go English' and make that our family's language."

I found it easy to be in a home where I did not have to censor my thoughts as well as my words. I was tired of hearing talk about "the Kaffirs" and "the niggers" and their supposed genetic inferiority to Whites. I was weary of being told that I don't understand, told that America is "the enemy" because we would slap economic sanctions on South Africa, warned that Communism is the monster at the door.

Every day since my arrival in South Africa I had reminded myself that I was a guest in the country, that I was a guest in the homes of South Africans who were going out of their way to be hospitable, and that I would have the courtesy to keep my mouth shut and listen. But the O'Neills were a family in which I did not have to keep my mouth so firmly closed. They were people who did not try to tell me what I was thinking, or what I *ought* to be thinking. They were genuinely interested in the opinion of an outsider coming to their country for the first time. They were rare.

I wished Terrence O'Neill a happy fiftieth birthday and hoped with all my heart that he and his family would be able to enjoy the rest of their days in the country they so obviously love.

VIII

DURBAN

I f you know something about Gandhi, the
▲ ▲ ▲ ▲ ▲ Indian leader who guided his people in
a doctrine of nonviolent civil disobedience, you know something about Durban. It was in this city that Gandhi began
his career among his countrymen at the turn of the century.

The first Indians arrived in Natal in 1860, recruited to work
on the sugar plantations that the British had begun to establish there. Those first laborers, mostly Hindus, came from
southern and eastern India, bound to work for the plantation
owners for three years (later that was extended to five years).
When they had finished their obligation, they had three options: they could renew their contracts, go back to India, or
take up farming themselves on a piece of crown land that
the government would give them. Most chose to stay.

These indentured servants, known as "immigrant Indians," were followed a few years later by so-called "passenger
Indians," who paid their own way to southern Africa. These

were people of a higher class, from northern and western India, mostly Muslim. They came to do business among the poorer immigrant Indians; eventually they made their way inland and established themselves as the merchant class. Ahmed Kumar, the schoolteacher in Cape Town, is descended from the passenger Indians. Most of South Africa's 800,000 Indians live in Natal, and most of those live in Durban.

But I did not meet any Indians in Durban. In fact I did not meet any English in Durban, something of a disappointment after hearing about the ODFs—Old Durban Families—and their legendary snobbishness. Instead I stayed with the Afrikaner family of a prominent businessman, who listened to my story of evasion and rudeness from educational bureaucrats who had so far managed to stymie all my attempts to get into an Afrikaans high school. He picked up the phone and called a friend, highly placed in government circles and a member of the Broederbond. This "brotherhood," a semisecret society founded in 1918 with the goal of promoting Afrikaner supremacy in all areas of South African life, has slowly gathered power over the years. Some view the exclusively male organization, meeting monthly in "circles" or cells, as a kind of sinister conspiracy. Sinister or not, the Broederbond wields a lot of influence, and it was this influence that finally opened the doors to an Afrikaner school.

"You will visit the school tomorrow," he said, putting down the phone. "And you will be treated with respect and courtesy."

The "Top Ten" Times Two

Everything had been superbly organized by the principal. I was to be at the high school at 11:45, and at precisely that moment a secretary ushered me into his office. His name,

132

carved on a wooden plaque on his desk, is J. M. K. de Klerk. Mr. de Klerk is a baldish man with a beard, heavy glasses, and a formal manner. He asked me to explain who I was and what I wanted, and then he told me what he had planned.

Mr. de Klerk had rounded up the "Top Ten," the ten best students from both Standard Eight and Standard Nine. These were not necessarily the gifted students, he said, although some are that, too, but the hardest working, the super-achievers of the school. They had a half-hour break before lunch at 12:30 and had agreed to meet with me during that period.

Mr. de Klerk escorted me to the meeting room. Someone had arranged the chairs in a square, a single chair on one side and twenty more forming the other three sides. The students had already arrived, boys on one side, girls on the other. After the greeting for which I was now prepared, he made a brief introduction. "I will leave you alone with them," he said, "but when you have finished, please report back to my office." When he left I wondered if I should salute.

Twenty students sat looking at me, waiting. I never know what to do with twenty students, or even ten. I would have preferred two or three, sitting over "cooldrinks" in a corner of the dining hall. This felt too much like a teacher/class situation, not my style. To get them to relax a little (to get *me* to relax a little), I told them something about my work, playing for laughs. I had heard that Afrikaner teachers never joke in the classroom, seldom stray from the subject, main-tain strictly formal relationships with their students. I de-cided as an American to break that barrier. The first anecdote to come to mind was the one about the Alaskan village where I had once gone to research a book about Eskimos. I described the unfamiliar foods I had eaten, raw fish and seal oil. "The equivalent of *boerewors* and biltong," I said. They smiled. Now what?

Next I tried going around the room and asking their names,

133

as I had in the Coloured primary school in Cape Town. I also asked them their main interests. Without exception, each one said "sport." Wasn't there one person here who preferred to play chess or sing in the chorus or act in plays? No. At least among the Top Ten, the crème de la crème of Afrikaner youth in Durban, it's sport.

"Why don't you ask *me* questions?" I suggested, thinking that would indicate what was on their minds, rather than imposing on them what was on mine. It worked. For students with the reputation of being passive sponges, soaking up whatever teacher says, these people were quick and keen and wasted no time in putting the hard questions.

A very tall blond boy named Christie van Wyck quickly emerged as the leader. It was he who established the line of questioning pursued by a few of the boys; the girls listened demurely. "What do Americans think of South Africa?"

"What do *you* think?"

"Does the reality of South Africa match your expectations?"

"Why is America so against us?"

"Don't you have apartheid too?"

"What about Harlem?"

"Why does the U.S. media portray us so badly, get everything twisted around?"

"Do you have any 'magical solutions' [said in ironic quotes] for our problems?"

I hedged a lot, determined not to lose my cool. I told them that I could in no way speak for 200 million Americans, nor could I speak for the government of my country. I confessed that I was having a hard time knowing, at that point, what *I* thought. I agreed that the problems were not simple. In my heart of hearts I believe it is simpler than they were willing to admit—that the only "magical solution" is to dismantle apartheid and share power with the Blacks. But my

134

"magical solution" is unacceptable to most White South Africans, and so—whether from politeness or cowardice—I said nothing. One more time, before we moved off the subject of politics, a boy named Robert said, "No one is going to tell us what to do."

Christie led us in another direction. "What's the difference between South African children and American 'kids'?" he asked, scratching the air to indicate quotation marks. "What about discipline?"

They have heard there is next to none in American schools. I spoke in favor of a balance between discipline and freedom, of the need to question and go beyond rote learning. They wanted to know what I thought about school uniforms. I told them I like the idea because it seems to cut down on the need to keep up or outdo. That reaction won me some points. We went on to punk styles, TV and movies, the relationship between parents and children in the United States (explain *that* in a few simple sentences!). Like the English letter writers in PMB, they believe there may be too much emphasis on sport in South Africa, but they justify it by saying it's one thing they can all do together. The rugged individualist is not much honored.

We had gone well over the allotted half-hour, cutting into their lunch period, but no one wanted to leave. I deliberately baited them with a mention of Desmond Tutu, the Black Anglican bishop of Johannesburg, winner of the 1984 Nobel Peace Prize, and highly controversial in his own country. He is not controversial among the Afrikaners; they can't stand him.

"He's Communist!" Christie stated flatly.

"How do you know?"

"He was on TV last week, standing in front of a Communist flag. If he's not a Communist, why was he in front of that flag?"

"Because your television presents things out of context, twists them around, just the way you say ours does."

J. M. K. de Klerk was waiting in his office with a cup of tea and a firm lecture on discipline. "Discipline is not punitive but is a highly organized structure. The Englishman," he said, "thinks freedom is *from* something, but the Afrikaner believes it is *for* something."

As we shook hands, Mr. de Klerk assured me that he has a superior education, is equally at home in English or Afrikaans, and is in no way like the uneducated Afrikaner in the street. "Please remind your countrymen that it is men like myself, men of my background and education, who are running South Africa."

Jean and Marta Roussouw

Prosperous Afrikaners in an English city, the Roussouws live on an estate about halfway between Durban and Pietermaritzburg and send their children to English private schools.

"Afrikaners graduating from government high schools do not make the marks they need for entrance into university," Marta Roussouw said flatly.

Afrikaner parents drive their children very hard to succeed, she claims, and she told me about a boy who placed very high in his matrics but who slept only four hours a night and spent the rest of the time at his books with no time off for anything else.

"I've told *my* children, there's more to life than high grades and studying," she said.

Their eldest daughter, Marie, is studying law in Cape Town, though she knows that she will have a rough time as a professional woman in this male-dominated society. Eugene, a gentle boy who keeps bees and is raising a cow in the back acres of his family's estate, is working toward a B.Com. degree (Bachelor of Commerce) at the University of Natal in Durban with the idea of someday joining his father's company. Minette, sixteen, and Jacques, thirteen, are both in English private schools, Jacques as a boarding student and Minette a day student whom Marta chauffeurs back and forth to school every day. Once a week Marta drops off a box of treats for Jacques, who looks every inch the English schoolboy in his gray flannel shorts, knee socks, crested blazer, and Eton cap.

The cost of maintaining such a family with a staff of six servants runs high, even for a man as successful as Jean. To make ends meet, Marta sews all the clothes for herself and her two daughters and operates a business making "everlastings," dried floral arrangements. Minette helps her. She has trained two of the servants to assemble the bouquets and wreathes, which are sold through some of the exclusive shops in the suburbs and downtown Durban. Her partner is a neighbor who also writes children's stories.

Their business operates at a loss, and the women are careful to keep it that way so their husbands can deduct the losses from their income taxes. The problem is, the writer told me, that since they don't make much money—although they could, if they wanted to and the men allowed it—their husbands do not have much regard for what they do. "If it doesn't make money, it's not valuable," the writer said. "He thinks my writing is a joke."

Jean is a distinguished-looking man with a thick mane of gray hair. The family revolves around him. First thing in the morning, while they are dressing for school, for university, for the office, one of the servants washes Jean's car, Marta's car, Eugene's *bakkie*. When Jean is ready, the maid serves breakfast in the dining room, Jean and Marta seated at opposite ends of a long stretch of polished mahogany.

Monday nights Jean gets his favorite dinner, beef stew,

which no one else likes; it is prepared out of deference to him. Marta shops carefully, watching out for Jean's consumption of red meat, cholesterol, salt, and other items that most Afrikaners take for granted. South Africa has the highest rate of heart disease in the world—one day of eating on the farm showed me why—but Marta has no intention of letting Jean become one of the statistics. She indulges his taste for beef with the Monday night stew, but otherwise she keeps him on poultry and fish, a decidedly un-Afrikaner diet. She wants him to quit smoking, but she smokes too.

Marta has no influence on his consumption of brandy. Early in the evening the bottle was brought to the lounge on a tray with a selection of drinks. Eugene and Minette watched television at the other end of the lounge, next to the fire, though I tried to coax them to join us. A couple of small dogs curled up on the sofa next to Marta. As the level of the brandy bottle went down, the level of Jean's belligerence went up. The first target of his irritation was Beatrice, the cook, a tall Zulu woman.

"Bloody savage," he snorted when she was barely out of the room. "Drank up my best wine."

Marta explained that Beatrice drinks quite a lot and regularly helps herself to their liquor supply. The last straw was when she drank all the expensive wines in Jean's cabinet. They have taken to hiding their good wines, but that evening when Jean dug out a bottle from among Marta's sewing supplies he discovered that it had gone bad from being stored improperly.

"Why don't you fire her?" I asked.

"Beatrice is intelligent and capable," Marta said. "All the bright ones drink, and the ones who don't drink are invariably stupid."

"Bloody Kaffir," Jean muttered, refilling his glass.

During the afternoon Marta had insisted on taking me to

a fake Zulu village of thatched huts, a tourist attraction that I would normally have avoided. We were the only visitors. We crawled inside the igloo-shaped huts, sat on logs, and listened to taped English explanations of the contents of the hut while a costumed Zulu pointed at the various cooking pots and other objects of daily life as the taped voice lectured on. The last stop was a small amphitheater where men in skins with rattles on their ankles and barebreasted girls danced for us. While we were shunted from one exhibit to the next, Marta chatted with the dancers and guides in Zulu. They were clearly impressed that she spoke their language so fluently—not just "Zulu for house and garden."

"I grew up speaking Zulu," she told me. "I know these people. Jean doesn't. He grew up in the city, and he didn't have the advantage of actually living with Blacks and getting to know them the way I do. When our children were little they learned Zulu first, because their nannies spoke to them in Zulu. I spoke Zulu to them as well. Jean couldn't even talk to them until they were five or six. That's why he is such a racialist."

The brandy gradually disappeared, and they discussed their servants. Marta justifies the low wages she pays by the fact that she supports a number of their relatives as well, people who live illegally in small houses on their property; according to law these people should be living out on the locations. Joshua, whom I have seen washing the cars, has been there for years, "doing less and less work every year," according to Jean. "When I offered to increase his wages in exchange for more work, just to get it back up to its former level, he refused."

Marta says Joshua has a traditional wife and ten children out in the country. Trying to persuade him to use some method of birth control, Marta has explained over and over to Joshua that there is only so much space on Planet Earth, which is now nearly filled to capacity. "Too many more people cannot survive here, I tell him." But Joshua does not think "globally," she says, and always responds to her lectures with one of his own: many children are a gift from God. A couple of generations ago in tribal villages they were not only a gift but a necessity.

To support his large family Joshua runs a shebeen on the Roussouws' property, an illegal liquor shop. Jean permits it, as long as there is no drunkenness. "Joshua makes quite a lot of money at it, and I help him keep track of it," Marta said. "The neighbors would have a fit if they knew."

Many Blacks take shortcuts across the Roussouws' land, because the road winds such a long way around. Some of their neighbors have tried to stop this traffic by building fences around their estates, but the Blacks immediately tunnel under them. The Roussouws laugh at their neighbors' naïveté; "Fences don't keep Blacks out," they said. "Might as well let them go through." They also leave their two cars and Eugene's *bakkie* unlocked, so that if anyone wants to steal a radio they will not break a window, which is expensive to replace and a nuisance, to get it. Probably as a result no one ever breaks into their cars, although their neighbors on both sides have their car windows smashed and their radios stolen fairly frequently.

The trick to survival, Marta said and Jean agreed, is to beat the system of ridiculous laws and high taxation by helping individual Blacks, letting them live on your property, letting them have their shebeens, and hoping you don't get caught.

But there is a limit to the help you can give them, the Roussouws say. Jean told the story of a Black law-school graduate whom a friend of his took on as articles clerk, a sort of apprentice in practical matters of law. The clerk was sent out to get a deposition from a witness, a written statement to be used in court. He came back with dozens of inconsequential details about every move he made on his way to the witness's home and concluded: "The witness was not there."

"That was all he needed to say," Jean said, " 'The witness was not there.' A deposition is what the witness says. But here is a law-school graduate who thinks a deposition is a record of every right and left turn he made on the way to find the witness. Hopeless! And my friend had taken on this man as a favor to me. I was embarrassed."

But Marta told another story, about the son of one of her sister's servants who also got a law degree but could not find a job. He ended up joining the police force, just to get some kind of work in order to repay his parents. But he was badly brutalized in the course of training—he wrote to Marta's sister about it, begging her not to tell his mother—and now has to leave his home with his uniform in a packet because policemen are hated in his neighborhood.

My answer to this, unspoken, was that these stories said nothing about the intelligence or ability of Blacks but a great deal about their education. Neither of these men, certainly, had received even a fraction of the education the Roussouws' daughter Marie was getting at Cape Town.

By the time the brandy bottle was down two-thirds, Jean had focused his hostility about the threat to his way of life that problems with the Blacks represent. He beamed that anger on the United States in general and on me in particular. My session at the Afrikaans high school had somewhat prepared me for the direction it would take. On the one hand, South Africans are astonished at the amount of attention they are receiving from the foreign press and television; on the other hand, they are surprised that they are not the center of attention all the time. Here I was again, playing diplomat, not wanting to offend my host who, after all, had arranged my visit to that school, or my hostess who had spent most of her day playing tour guide.

"If America loses her morality, the whole world is lost,"

Jean said through a thick fog of brandy. "And it is up to you, Carolyn. It is up to the mothers, the teachers, the writers to remind America of her moral position."

I was not sure what he was talking about, except that I figured it had to do with economic sanctions against South Africa, then being debated in the Congress of the United States. Putting a financial squeeze on South Africa would mean, in Jean Roussouw's thinking, that America had lost her morality. And Jean seemed convinced that the mothers, teachers, and writers could stop this outrage.

I thought he was placing the responsibility where it did not belong. The politics of South Africa has to do with money, privilege, and power, and I said so.

"Bloody Yank," he yelled. "You're a bloody Yank! You won't be satisfied until you've destroyed everything and given the whole country to the Communists!"

I had had enough. I was tired of being a target. "And you're a dumb bloody Dutchman," I roared back. "We're natural enemies. Let's just drop it."

I did not sleep much that night. The next morning we met again at that polished mahogany table over boxes of fiber cereal provided by Marta to save her husband from heart attack. Jean wore a three-piece pinstriped suit and his most urbane manner.

"You must come back," he said. "You know nothing at all about South Africa. You should come and stay here for six months, a year. Then maybe you would know something. Maybe you would understand. You are always welcome as our guest." He bowed politely.

I thanked him, just as politely. And left.

PART FOUR

Not in South Africa

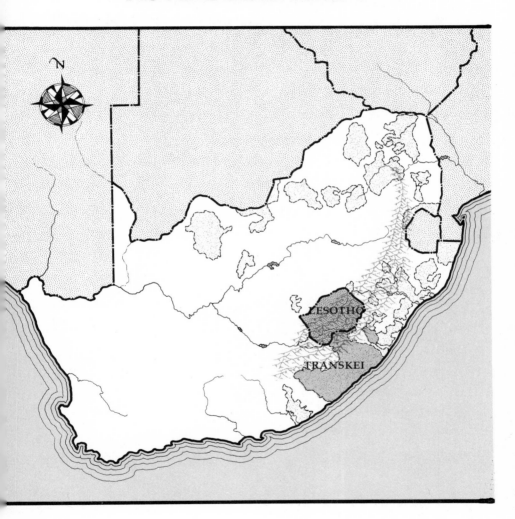

IX

TRANSKEI

Ringing out from our blue heavens,
    from our deep seas breaking round;
Over everlasting mountains
    where the echoing crags resound.
From our plains where creaking wagons
    cut their trails into the earth—
Calls the spirit of our country,
    of the land that gave us birth.
At thy call we shall not falter,
    firm and steadfast we shall stand,
At thy will to live or perish,
    O South Africa, dear land.

▲ ▲ ▲ ▲ ▲ T hat is the first stanza of "Die Stem van Suid-Afrika" (The Call of South Africa), the national anthem. The *White* national anthem. For millions of South Africans who are not White, "the land that gave us birth" might indeed have been South African soil and South Africa their "dear land," but they cannot claim South African citizenship. These are the millions of Blacks whom the government has assigned to one of the "homelands."

145

According to the Official Yearbook of the Republic of South Africa, "The Black States Citizenship Act of 1970 gave every Black man, regardless of where he lived, the opportunity of becoming a citizen of his state of origin. He would exercise his political rights in his national state, but he would not be an alien in South Africa until his state became independent." What the yearbook does not say is that the Black man (and the Black woman) has no choice in the matter; it is not "opportunity"—it is law. Whether he (or she) wants it or not, every Black in South Africa is assigned citizenship, on the basis of the language the person speaks, in one of the "homelands" set aside by the government, even if that person has never set foot there.

During the 1950s the White government of South Africa hit upon a solution to the problem of what to do with the Black population that was growing at a faster rate than the Whites, and already far outnumbered them. They could not simply abandon the country to the Blacks, and integrating them meant being swamped by the vast numbers. Their ingenious solution was "separate development"; Whites would set up separate systems of government and administration for Blacks, so the Blacks could, in theory at least, become autonomous and responsible for their own affairs. Nobody ever suggested that "separate" should also be "equal"—just different.

To make this idea work, the government would create isolated areas called homelands, where Blacks would be forced to live, except when their labor was needed in the mines, on the farms, or somewhere else. The White government based its "multinational" scheme on the fact that Black Africans come from a variety of tribal backgrounds, reflected by their variety of languages—Xhosa, Zulu, Sotho, Tswana, Venda, and others. These were all quite different cultures, the officials insisted, and in fact tribal rivalries were so fierce that they had to be kept separate. They *preferred* the separation,

146

the theory went, so they could live peacefully in places where other tribes would not try to dominate them. Each tribe in its own "nation state" could achieve its true destiny, politically, economically, culturally. Naturally no one consulted the Blacks; they were simply told what to do.

And so the government put together ten homelands, originally called Bantustans until the derogatory term "Bantu" went out of fashion. To create a homeland, scattered fragments of land were grouped together and given a name. The government maintains that the fragmentation was not the result of any attempt by the Whites to preserve the best lands for themselves, "but by history." Blacks had originally settled in these areas of their own choice, looking for water and grazing land and also for a buffer strip to separate their tribe from the others. Gradually the government acquired more small parcels and added them to the original pockets of land, until there were about two hundred fragments divided up among ten homelands. Even after some consolidation only one of the ten—tiny Qwaqwa—consists of a single chunk. The division as well as the number, ten, is said by the government's critics to be completely arbitrary.

Roughly 13 percent of the land in South Africa has been set aside as Black homelands. Most of it is the poorest land in the country. Seventy-two percent of the population of South Africa is Black. (The 12 percent Coloured and Asian are not assigned to homelands.) About half of the Black population now lives on the homelands—around ten million people, a figure that has more than doubled in the past twenty years. Theoretically all Blacks are citizens there, although they are allowed to work where they are needed, divided between White farms and White cities. What this all adds up to is that 36 percent of the total number of people in South Africa are now living on 13 percent of the country's land, most of it unproductive. Eighty percent of the people in the homelands, roughly eight million, live below poverty level.

Over fifty thousand children are believed to die each year of hunger in South Africa, most of them in the homelands.

Homelands are sad places, dry, dusty, and poor. The people already living there struggle to survive; those shipped out from the cities add to the misery. A plan to set up "border industries" that would employ citizens of the homelands has not been successful. Newcomers dumped in the homelands have no work, no income, no decent place to live, no way to feed themselves and their children. They scheme to get back to the cities, where at least there is a chance of finding work—but where they will invariably end up living in wretched squatters' camps, trying to elude the police who will arrest them, send them to jail, and then banish them to the homeland again. Many are willing to risk arrest and jail. They can slip illegally into a city, work for three months, spend nine months in jail, and still have more than double the money at the end of the twelve months that they would have earned in a year in the homeland.

In 1963 the Transkei, a homeland for speakers of Xhosa and Sotho located along the Indian Ocean between East London and Durban, was granted full internal self-government. In 1976 in the eyes of the White bureaucracy it had reached its maximum potential of "separate development" and became a sovereign state, the Republic of Transkei, with its own flag and its own national anthem. Since then three more homelands have achieved "independence": Bophuthatswana, Venda, and Ciskei. The six others—Qwaqwa, Gazankulu, KwaZulu, KwaNdebele, KaNgwane, and Lebowa —splattered on the map of South Africa like a skin disease, have "internal self-government" but not yet independence.

Most of the homelands are ruled by leaders hand-picked by the South African government. Independence is an illusion, and not even a very good fake, since the homelands are totally dependent economically on South Africa and must take orders from there. Some, like KwaZulu, under the leadership of Gatsha Buthelezi (GAHT-shuh boo-tuh-LAY-zee), have rejected the idea of such independence. The only country that recognizes the "independent national states" is South Africa. No other nation in the world accepts them. The goal of the White government is to make as many Blacks as possible "foreigners," citizens of foreign countries invented by South Africa. These foreigners, of course, have no political role anywhere but in their homelands and are no longer a political threat.

But there is one success story. Bophuthatswana (BO-pooh-that-SWAH-nuh) is a handful of fragments scattered across the northern Transvaal with a few pieces in the northern Cape and the eastern Free State. Most chunks lie near the Botswana border, but one glittering shard is within a couple of hours' drive of Johannesburg.

The main attraction in that plot of dusty land in the middle of nowhere is Sun City, a miniature Las Vegas featuring all the things forbidden in South Africa; gambling, for instance—slot machines and roulette wheels and blackjack games; porno films; and (until the ban was recently lifted in South Africa) interracial couples. There is an indoor amphitheater featuring musical extravaganzas with glitzy costumes and chorus lines. Top stars from the United States have been lured on stage there—Dolly Parton and Liza Minelli and Frank Sinatra (who was said to gross $1.4 million for two weeks of appearances). Many American entertainers have agreed not to perform in South Africa because of its apartheid laws, but they feel that Sun City is "different"; they have been persuaded that it is truly an independent homeland and segregation laws are not in effect. Sun City is heavily advertised in Johannesburg. Not only tourists looking for a wilder time than Johannesburg has to offer but South Africans as well fill the tour buses or drive up for a big night out.

The result is that the Republic of Bophuthatswana is raking

in a lot of money, a percentage of everything brought into Sun City. Besides that revenue, Bophuthatswana also has platinum mines, all controlled by South Africa. But this wealth has not affected the daily life of most of the Tswana, the people who live there, many of them unemployed. Of those who have jobs, two-thirds have to travel long distances every day into South Africa to work.

The Republic of Transkei is a homeland that is not a success story, though it was once thought to have a chance. Since it is a genuine center of Xhosa culture, and not a made-up one, the British had considered making it an independent country. The yearbook claims that the per capita income of Transkei is growing faster than that of any other Black African country. In 1976 the residents were instructed to vote on a referendum to determine whether or not their homeland should be declared an independent nation-state. The chief minister of Transkei silenced his opponents by locking them up until the voting was over, to guarantee "independence." He turned out to be even more harsh in his rule than the Whites from whom he learned his techniques. He clamped the Transkei under a continual state of emergency and banned students and other possible opponents, allowing them to leave their homes only to attend school or go to church.

On the Road to Umtata

Brenda, the clerk in the rental car office back in Stellenbosch, thought I was crazy; she would not dream of driving across South Africa alone. Mary McChesney, the woman who showed no qualms at taking me into the Coloured townships of Cape Town, had said I was asking for trouble. I was nervous about driving on the left side of the road, an unfamiliar car in an unfamiliar country. I wasn't sure, either, where I might run into trouble—people throwing rocks, setting tires alight on the roads. They would see that I was White, alone, vulnerable. There would be no time, if they came after me, to brandish my American passport. But buses ran on twice-a-week schedules, trains seemed not to go where I wanted, and there were no airports in some of the places I planned to stop. Driving was the only way to see the country. The professor in Stellenbosch was sure I would be perfectly safe, and that was what I wanted to hear. He marked a map for me, and his wife escorted me to the edge of town. I gripped the wheel and tried to get the knack of shifting gears with my left hand.

After a while I relaxed. The scenery was spectacular: baboons loping near the highway, ostriches strutting behind fences, the lovely Tzitzikama Forest, my first sight of the Indian Ocean. But the road got more difficult as the day wore on, with detours and construction work. In my zeal for keeping left I hit a marker by the side of the road and blew a tire. A man in a *bakkie* stopped to change it for me. I kept on going and got to Grahamstown on schedule. So far, so good. Except for the tire, no problems.

But my next scheduled stop was Umtata, the capital of Transkei, and suddenly I was uneasy. I had been warned to be *very careful* in Transkei. There would be animals all over the road: goats skitter out of the way when you hit the "hooter" but sheep stop dead and cows move implacably onward. To hit one could mean real trouble. People walk along the sides of the road, sometimes stepping unexpectedly out into your path.

But I was also uneasy about being a White person alone in a Black country. South Africa, in my mind, is a White country under White law, even though Blacks far outnumber Whites. But I understand White culture, or at least I *think* I

151

do. And now I was going into a Black country, and I did not know if the rules would be different. If I accidentally hit a goat in South Africa, I was fairly sure that South African law would take the side of a White American tourist. But suppose that happened in Transkei? I had already proved that I could run into a stationary object; it was certainly not out of the question that I might hit a bounding little goat. Would they put me in jail?

I passed through the homeland named Ciskei with only a wave from a uniformed Black man at the border post, but entering Transkei was a formal occasion. The border station is large and the number of officials seemed more than necessary. With their multiple forms and profusion of stamps they were not particularly efficient, but they were polite. Checking documents at the border might be one of the main sources of employment in this poor country.

It seemed like a long way to Umtata, where I had the security of a reservation in a Holiday Inn. But in the meantime I didn't stop for food or gas or anything else, even in a lively town named Butterworth that sounded terribly British and reminded me of American pancakes. I just kept on driving, too afraid of being the only White woman on the street or in a restaurant and annoyed at myself for feeling that way. This is the situation White South Africans live with all the time. It helped me understand their fear of a Black-dominated country and their determination to stay in control.

The scenery was uniformly brown and dry, the signs of deep erosion unmistakable. The land has been vastly over-grazed. Where once there had been immense herds of cattle, now only goats can survive. Some of them are Angora, imported for their long, silky mohair. But the goats are devastating the landscape. They don't just nibble the plants down to the ground, as sheep and cattle do; they pull them out, chew the leaves off bushes, eventually destroying the cover.

"If there were one thing I could do for Africa," one man told me, "it would be to get rid of the goats. Wherever there are goats, desert follows, and that's true all over the world, not just in Africa."

The highways were crowded—not with cars but with animals and pedestrians, many of them heading big loads. They held out their thumbs half-heartedly, not really expecting a ride. Occasionally I passed a donkey cart or a man on horseback.

I drove through villages, clusters of rectangular buildings or round mud huts called rondavels with cone-shaped thatched roofs. Women were cutting tall grass for thatch along the road. It was the time of year for building and repairing houses, before the spring rains began, before the new green growth replaced the dried blond grasses. Houses, both round and square, were partially painted, leaving the plain mud intentionally exposed. (I never could find out why, except that it was the custom.) The paint was always the same bilious green.

On the outskirts of Umtata I stopped at a "crafts center" filled with all kinds of souvenirs, mostly junk, sporting bright orange labels reading "Bought in Transkei." Except for the bead necklaces and mohair shawls and blankets, I'd guess most of it had been made somewhere in Asia. I was the only customer until a tour bus pulled in and disgorged a horde of tired, disgruntled Australian tourists. I crept on to the refuge of the Holiday Inn.

Most of the guests were Black, most of them businessmen in smart suits. I ordered afternoon tea in the lobby—I was now completely hooked on this custom—and watched the people come and go. Then the tour bus arrived with the Australians, laden with souvenirs and luggage and complaining loudly. I hoped no one would mistake my accent for theirs.

Mrs. Ngani

Mrs. Ngani walks like a queen. A tall, elegant woman with classic African features, full lips, broadly flaring nostrils, her long skull accentuated by the way she draws her hair into a tight knot, she probably does come from a line of chiefs. She is a member of Umtata's upper middle class, her husband in the top level of the Transkei government. Mrs. Ngani teaches English in the high school.

If they were Whites in South Africa, in the nearby coastal town of East London, for instance, the Nganis would have a fine home, a garden with a swimming pool, a couple of servants, a BMW if not a Mercedes. But they are Blacks in a Black homeland. She drove me past their home, a modest house on a pleasant street checkerboarded with White homes. "Some Whites who live in Umtata for business reasons adjust to nonsegregated living better than others," she said. "Those from the Transvaal seem to have the worst time."

The one thing the Nganis do strive for, the one thing they have in common with their White counterparts elsewhere, is that their children are all in private schools of some kind —a son who graduated from a boarding school in Grahamstown, a daughter in another school there (it was her headmaster, Mr. Peterson, who gave me Mrs. Ngani's name), the youngest boy in a pre-primary group run by a White woman in her Umtata home. They have strained their resources to the limit to buy a White education for their children, knowing it is vastly superior to the education normally available to Blacks.

Mrs. Ngani's middle son, Mitchell, is a pupil at the Vela School (*vela* means "to rise and grow" in Xhosa), a private school for Black children. It now runs through Standard Two—fourth grade—but Mrs. Ngani dreams that someday Vela School will be a boarding school with a swimming pool and tennis courts, just like the White schools. When she drove me there in her battered Toyota, the children from the primary grades were lined up outside a small building for their toilet break. This, I thought, must surely be different from White schools.

We went into one of the classrooms. The children were dressed in bright blue uniforms trimmed in white. Some had jackets with the school name embroidered on the pocket. The class rose and went through the ritual greeting. The teachers in this Black school are Coloured. "Most Blacks never get enough education to qualify as top-flight teachers," Mrs. Ngani explained. "Very few have a university degree or even a matric. The education available to Coloureds is better. So we hired Coloured teachers."

The property, which had been donated to the school, reaches all the way to the river in the distance and includes several buildings once used as guest houses. They look rather shabby on the outside, but inside they are bright and cheerful with curtains at the windows, new desks (always shared by two pupils), pictures on the walls, and carefully lettered charts above the chalkboards. Some classrooms have cozy corners with carpet and floor cushions where the children gather for certain kinds of instruction. New rooms are being added, plans are on the books to paint the buildings, and a workman is spading up the earth to plant small gardens.

Five children now in Standard Two have been pupils at the school since its beginnings in another place, and they gathered on the verandah to have their picture taken. There was hesitation and whispering, though, that for once had nothing to do with my camera fiddling; the row of book satchels lined up outside the classroom door seemed "untidy," and they wanted to move them. I had to convince them that the satchels really belonged in the picture.

We settled down to talk, four girls—Ncumisa, Eza, Anda,

and Luntu—and one boy, Chuma. They were all nine years old, but tomorrow would be Anda's tenth birthday. Anda, taller than the others, has big ears and wears glasses. Saturday her family would invite about forty relatives and friends for a birthday party, she said proudly. They'd have a chocolate cake and sweets (candy). Her wish was for a little tape player with earphones. When I asked the others what they would like for their birthdays, the girls mentioned a bedspread, a pretty dress, school supplies. Chuma, the boy, wished for a motorbike.

The conversation switched to Christmas, when they said the custom was to hang a sock by the bed for presents. Some of the families drive to the beach—the beautiful "Wild Coast" is only an hour or so away on the Indian Ocean—but Anda said primly that her father always waits until after Christmas to make the trip, when crowds are smaller and accidents are fewer.

Mrs. Ngani signaled that it was time to leave. She was due at the high school for her own classes. There was a chorus of farewells from the Standard Twos.

I asked her about school boycotts on the way back to the Holiday Inn. "Sometimes it is necessary to destroy everything in order to build up something new," she said. "Among the Blacks the parents have become like children, following orders, and the children are seizing political power. They are forcing things to happen. If the children were not destroying the schools, if things were to return to normal, the government would not make any changes. We must be prepared to make sacrifices in order to move ahead."

Then I asked her opinion of economic sanctions, much discussed in the United States at that time. "Won't it hurt the Blacks, the very ones it's supposed to help?" I asked, repeating the argument of conservative Whites.

"It is like the boycotts," she explained patiently. "Of course it will harm some Blacks in the short run, but it is a necessary

156

evil. It will put pressure on the Whites, and they are the ones who have the most to lose. Most Blacks have nothing to lose, and the rest understand the need to sacrifice."

I asked Mrs. Ngani to take me to visit her English class at Umtata High School, but she was not encouraging. It was very complicated to get permission, she said; I would have to make an official application, and that would take time. Besides, there had been trouble recently. She promised to call me that evening; perhaps her husband would know others I could meet. But I did not hear from her again.

Paul and Kaya

"Bomb?"

"Yes, Madam. We've had a report of a bomb in this building. I must ask you to follow me."

I didn't ask any more questions; I stumbled through the kitchen of the teachers' cafeteria, down a passageway, and into bright sunlight. The two Black university students followed me.

"Does this happen often?" I asked when we were a safe distance from the threatened building, standing around with the others who had been evacuated. Nobody seemed particularly frightened.

"It is part of our education," the student named Paul said, laughing.

"Black education is always being interrupted by *something*," Kaya added.

We were outside the University of Transkei, a cluster of modern buildings across the highway from the Holiday Inn. I had wandered around the compact campus, looking for somebody to talk to. I had no appointment there, no contacts; I just went.

A secretary in one of the administrative offices saw me in

the hall, looking lost, trying to figure out the best place to start. When I told her who I was, she made a few phone calls and then led me through a maze of elevators and walkways to another building and the office of the guidance counselor, someone she thought might be able to collar a couple of students.

Miss Lusu is a pretty young woman with a nice smile. She wore jeans, and her office walls are decorated with Snoopy posters. While she went looking for students, I scanned her bookshelves. All the books are in English, most by American authors with names familiar in the world of popular psychology, on the subjects of loving and being your own best friend.

It was Paul who reluctantly agreed to take a break. He excused his reluctance saying he had too much work to do; I felt it was because he really did not want to talk to me. Paul led me to the cafeteria, where I offered to buy him lunch. He settled for a glass of fruit juice. Then Kaya came to join us, sent by Miss Lusu.

Paul was in his second year at the university, studying botany and zoology. Kaya was a first-year student, repeating it because last year there were also "troubles" and he could not write his exams. (Kaya, pronounced KY-uh, means "house" in Xhosa; there is no vocabulary of common names in African languages, and children can be named anything at all that the parents like.) Kaya was studying accounting and other business subjects for a B.Com. He wants to work in a bank or business, "But who knows?" he asked with a shrug. Paul has no idea where his degree will take him. Major-switching is common among Black university students, he said, because of "problems with certain subjects"—such as whether or not they will be available. Kaya admitted that he is depressed about his future. Having to repeat a year of study because of boycotts and bomb scares would be enough to discourage even the most determined.

The university's men's dormitories had been closed for several weeks, an action taken by government and school authorities because they fear having groups of young men living together. The women's hostels were still open; girls, they said, don't get politically involved.

I asked what the issues were in this so-called independent republic. They told me that some weeks earlier there had been a peaceful protest, and the protesters had been arrested. When sympathetic students attended the trial of the protesters, those students were themselves detained. Now a large group was in jail, and Paul and Kaya and others had had to find someplace else to stay in Umtata as well as transportation to the campus, located several miles from downtown. Kaya, whose home is in Queenstown over the Transkei border in the eastern Cape, was staying with relatives; Paul, from Johannesburg, shuttled from place to place. The housing problem was solved temporarily, but both of them complained that they were not able to study alone, without other students. The cooperative element was missing.

Waiting for the building to blow up or not, I asked them about violence involving the death of Blacks at the hands of other Blacks, as about a third of them are reported to be.

"Is it tribal?"

They said no. They denied, for instance, that a Zulu policeman would beat up a Xhosa student because Zulus hate Xhosas, a favorite White theory. But Kaya's theory is that Black parents habitually strike their children as a disciplinary measure, and that the accepted way for one to show authority over another is to beat him. Hence there is nothing strange about a Black policeman using a sjambok on a Black student; the policeman is acting in the role of a parent. The students reject this relationship of superior/parent/policeman to inferior/child/student and want to sit down and talk things out, but the police continue to beat them, and the students continue to fight back.

159

Kaya was worried about my safety. "You need someone with you," he said.

"What kind of person?" I asked him.

"A White man," he said. "In some places, like Cape Town, hostile Blacks might want to stone you even though you're sympathetic. They don't know how you feel; they only know that your skin is white. If I tried to protect you, to explain you to them, they would also try to kill me."

Angry young Blacks are quick to punish any Black they suspect of being a collaborator, a quisling, an informer, and they mete out their harsh brand of justice swiftly, accounting for many of the dead. This is not, after all, a court of law. It is war, and it makes the blood run cold.

"Jesus needs to come down here *now*," Kaya said fervently.

"He is overdue," Paul said.

The Children of Ngqeleni

The highway out of the Umtata passes through settlements called kraals, a collection of the thatched mud houses known as rondavels. To construct a rondavel, a circle of poles is set in the ground and interwoven with vines, like a basket; layers of mud are built up over the framework. There is a primitive dignity to these kraals. Along the road women headed heavy burdens: the poles for the rondavels, the thatch cut along the roadside, the family laundry on its way to a spring where groups of women chatted as they rubbed the clothes clean. They walk miles, these Xhosa, miles to do the wash, miles to go to school.

On one side of the highway, plainly marked with road signs, is the village of Libode, a collection of rundown houses with a general store on the main street. Before Transkei became an "independent republic" ten years ago, there was a large White population, most of whom have since moved away. Some Whites stay on in Umtata, surviving life in a country with a ten o'clock curfew every night (violators may be shot) by commuting to the Wild Coast on weekends. But there are no Whites in Libode any more. Now most of the houses there have Black owners, who can't afford or don't bother to maintain them. Libode has a sadly derelict air.

But on the other side of the highway a steep and rutted road dips into a valley and then climbs up a hillside to a kraal visible in the distance. I had heard there was a school there, and I decided to drop in for a visit, without the formal application, without the customary red tape. I headed for the kraal.

The children, apparently out for recess or perhaps alerted by some sort of grapevine, crowded against the fence as I bounced over the rough road, past women tending pots over a fire outside a rondavel. The women looked up in surprise and smiled as I rattled by, but the children were much more excited. They cheered and waved as I managed to get the car turned around in the narrow road without ending up in a ditch and parked it by the fence.

"Good morning, children!" I called out, having now learned my lines.

"Good morning, Madam!"

"Will you take me to your principal?"

"Yes, Madam!"

Fortunately Madam found an opening in the fence and did not have to crawl over or through it. "Okay, let's go."

"Let's go!" they chorused.

We started across the schoolyard with me at the head of the parade of two dozen pupils. The mud buildings needed a new coat of whitewash and the doors and window frames could have used some paint, but the grounds were immaculate, the dirt paths carefully swept and outlined with whitewashed stones. A rusty tire rim suspended from a tree limb served as a gong to call children to class.

The principal did not look at all surprised to see me. A small Black man in a frayed but spotless shirt, he listened politely to my explanation of who I was and what I wanted and introduced me to a woman teacher much taller than either of us. They discussed the situation in Xhosa and told me they would arrange for me to talk to some of the children. But first they must arrange a space in one of the classrooms.

The principal rounded up a couple of boys to carry a table and chairs into one of the rooms. Students passed by staring, the girls shy and retiring, the boys showing off with a little jive. There were lots of smiles, warm and friendly. Then someone fetched a plastic cover for the table, and at last I was led inside with three nervous girls who had been drafted to talk to me.

It was dark inside the classroom—there is no electricity, and the Xhosa are not fond of large windows—and it took me a while to adjust to the dim light. The walls were made of thick mud, set with a couple of tiny windows and a crooked wooden door. The floors were mud. The peak roof was made of corrugated metal supported by saplings. A piece of slate was propped on a crude easel. Apparently I had interrupted a chemistry class: there were two glass milk bottles filled with unknown substances, and an explanation of the diffusion of molecules was written in careful script on the blackboard. Plastic sacks of books and other items were stowed under the rough desks. No leather satchels here.

Thandiwe (tahn-DEE-wee), seventeen, is in Standard Seven and lives in Umtata but comes out from the city by bus. Her English was not good enough to explain why she does not attend school in town, and I did not know how to ask the right questions. Kutala, thirteen, Standard Five, told me that she is one of ten children and lives on the other side of the

162

highway in Libode. Her father, a policeman in Ciskei, comes home only once a year. Most children in Transkei and the other homelands have absentee fathers who work far away, many in the mines near Johannesburg. Zukiswa, sixteen, Standard Seven, lives in a rondavel in this kraal, called Ngqeleni, an unpronounceable name with two "clicks." She has no father; her mother supports the five children by sewing clothes, which she sells locally. Zukiswa helps her cut the cloth with a pattern, and her mother sews it on a hand-operated sewing machine.

Zukiswa and Kutala say they want to be nurses, a dream cherished by many Black girls. But when they finish Standard Seven here they will have to go to Umtata to the high school, and the bus fare may be prohibitive. Then there is the problem of finding the money to continue. While we talked, struggling with English, the principal sat quietly in a corner, observing but not entering into the conversation.

Out in the schoolyard several boys batted a ball around with flag-shaped wooden paddles.

"What are you playing?" I asked them as I was leaving.

"Tennis!"

X

LESOTHO

▲▲▲▲▲ "You really ought to see Lesotho," said Edward Hall, a salesman from Bloemfontein who deals in whatever he thinks Blacks will buy. "It's completely different from the Transkei."

There was no compelling professional reason for me to go to Lesotho, the small independent Black kingdom stuck in the middle of South Africa which shares borders with Transkei, Natal, the Cape, and the Orange Free State. About the time the first English settlers were planting their feet in Grahamstown, a Sotho chief named Moshesh was fighting off not only the Zulu raiders but also the Boers. In 1868 he put his people under British protection, and in 1884 Basutoland, as it was then called, came under the direct control of Britain. Its land area is 11,716 square miles (somewhat larger than the state of New Hampshire) with a population of 1.5 million.

At one time plans were made to incorporate Basutoland

into what was to be South Africa, but the Sotho would have none of it—especially when apartheid became the law of that land. In 1966 Basutoland became the independent Lesotho (pronounced leh-SOO-too), then-reigning King Moshoeshoe II went into exile, and the current prime minister dispatched with bullets hundreds of members of the political party that opposed his leadership.

Edward Hall travels this territory, driving the standard white Mercedes and dressing in three-piece suits, because he knows that is what his customers expect. On this trip he planned to peddle cheap plastic dishes to shops in Maseru, the capital of Lesotho. Then Edward would roam through the hinterlands to sell, of all things, calendars with pretty pictures to be imprinted with the name of the local business. He thought I should go along, to see what a truly independent Black African state was like, how it would differ from Transkei. The capital of the Free State is an hour and a half by car from Maseru. Edward offered to drive me there.

The road from Bloemfontein crosses the borders of a stray fragment of Bophuthatswana with only small signs to mark the crossings. But entry into Lesotho required a search of the car and surly questions from border guards.

Once upon a time Maseru was a booming casino resort center with a seven-hundred-room Holiday Inn sporting a gigantic freeform swimming pool, an outdoor bar, and lush gardens. But then the homelands were created, and White South Africans looking for a place to raise a little hell began going north to Sun City and east to the Wild Coast of the Transkei. Now the fancy hotel swimming pool is empty (partly a result of the ongoing drought which has reached disaster proportions) and so are most of the seven hundred rooms. Holiday Inn no longer owns the hotel; it is now called the Maseru Casino Inn and the lobby is furnished with slot machines. A few bored people pull the levers.

Across from the walled compound of the American Embassy is the walled compound of a cabinet minister. There I waited in the car while Edward made his first call of the day, an attempt to collect a debt from the minister. He was not optimistic.

The minister's house is built of stone with a metal roof, a nonluxurious dwelling with an Audi 5000 and a Mercedes sedan parked behind it. A constant stream of trucks drove in and out of the dusty yard. Men came and went, some of them draped in the traditional Sotho blanket with its colorful large-scale designs. Some stood idly dipping into bowls of mealie pap.

Then I noticed something I had not seen in South Africa: guns. An elegant man in a flashy suit and well-polished shoes pulled up in a black BMW and strolled casually into the minister's house carrying an AK-47, a military rifle.

The longer Edward was in that house, the more anxious I became. An hour went by. Longer. When Edward came out at last, he had a postdated check for the full amount, but he was fairly certain the check would bounce. The minister had kept him waiting while he ate breakfast, a pistol next to his plate. He belched noisily during their meeting.

We drove out of Maseru on a detour, a corduroyed dirt road that shook the Mercedes unmercifully. It was a dry, bleak landscape, erosion out of control, goats cavorting. A troop of boys passed wrapped in blankets, their faces coated in white clay, their heads topped with straw headpieces. They were initiates going through their "school." While we drove, Edward told me stories. Had I noticed, for instance, that rural Blacks wear layer upon layer of clothing, even in the warmest weather? That is because they believe the additional layers protect them from the sun. He also claims that Blacks don't drink red wine because when they drink red wine and pass yellow urine, they believe the red is still inside them somewhere.

From there he went through a number of "van der Merwe jokes," ethnic jokes of which Afrikaners are the butt (told by the English, of course). I never seemed to get them, although I did understand the van der Merwe mug with the handle *inside* the cup. The caricature of van der Merwe as a stupid lout did not fit the van der Merwes I had met, or any other Afrikaners.

The road led through the villages of Teyateyaneng (he calls it "T-Y"), Leribe, and finally to Butha Buthe, where Edward called on local businesses, promoting his line of calendars. I sat in on one of his spiels to the owner of a hotel and restaurant. I could hardly imagine how such a business survived in such an impoverished village, let alone spent money for advertising giveaways.

The hotel keeper, who never removed his felt hat, paid close attention to Edward's pitch, that an attractive calendar would make a distinctive gift for the hotel's select clientele. The owner's wife came out of the kitchen to help in the choice of styles. Top of the line had a number of large photographs of scenic splendors of the world—the Swiss Alps, for instance. Another series had cute pictures of animals; the one that particularly appealed to the wife was a blue-eyed, blond-haired child feeding a white lamb with a baby's bottle. But both roared with laughter at the calendar with the pictures of chimpanzees dressed up in clothes and engaged in human activities. The hotel owner ordered some of each. I watched in amazement and some dismay as Edward wrote up a sale that would have been sizable in a U.S. city. After that I preferred to remain in the car or to wander around with my little camera, snapping pictures of giggly girls who were not too shy to ask for money.

Outside a market several women sat nursing their babies in the sunshine. When her baby had been fed, one woman stood up, bent forward and, holding the child by one chubby arm, deftly swung it over her shoulder so that it lay sprawled across her back. Then she wrapped a blanket around it, tying two ends across her chest above her breasts and two ends below. The baby was secure, its bright face peering out above the blanket. Although it was a warm day, the mother added another blanket, pinning that one across her chest as well, all but covering the baby's face. Finally she picked up a large wooden crate of tomatoes and balanced it on her head. The other women arranged their infants the same way, heading one load and leaving their hands free for additional things. They moved off serenely down the dusty street.

Edward was in a fine mood as we headed back to Maseru. Business had been good and so were his commissions. Then we noticed soldiers standing on ridges above the highway, holding AK-47s; roadblock ahead. I tried to imagine how I would have dealt with this if I had been driving alone. Edward was ordered to open the trunk of his car (the "boot") and to reveal the contents of his sample cases. The soldiers stared at me, shrunk into a corner of the front seat. Across the road a bus had been stopped, and the passengers were being lined up and body searched. The soldiers accepted Edward's explanation of who I was—"An American lady, writing books for children"; they never asked me—and waved us on.

Downtown Maseru has a business district with a few decent shops and a couple of not-bad restaurants. An American accent in a craft shop grabbed my ear. I was buying thick sheepskin slippers and little clay cows, both typical of the area, when I heard her voice. "What are *you* doing here?" I asked her, probably sounding as though I thought I was the only American ever to venture to such a remote spot.

"Peace Corps," she said. A woman in her early sixties, Dorothy said her job is to get the craft center operating on a businesslike basis. "I love it here. I feel needed, a lot more than I did back home in Phoenix. I have a real pretty house up in the mountains, but the security is bad there and they moved me into town." South African terrorists are known to hide out in Lesotho, and every now and then the South African security police storm across the border and seize anyone they suspect. I was not sure if Dorothy's security problems were due to the terrorists or the South Africans who had come to bag them—or both.

Visitors to Maseru—like the man from Zimbabwe who was there to supervise the planting of grass seed at the new "international airport"—gathered at the town's other luxury hotel to play roulette in the casino or to bowl tenpins in the alleys below the lobby. I preferred bowling, but I developed a wretched left hook on my ball which I blamed on trying to bowl south of the Equator where everything, like water swirling down the drain, is backwards. You have to blame something.

I flew on to Johannesburg out of the old Maseru airport, since the new "international" one with the grass was not yet operational. The twin-engine aircraft was of some ancient vintage that worried me a little. Before we boarded, passengers were taken one by one into small curtained booths. I presented my American passport and was courteously ushered on through, but when one of the curtains flapped open I realized that other passengers were being body searched; my U.S. passport had protected me. There have been times traveling in other countries that I have clutched my blue booklet stamped "United States of America" like a holy book. This was one of those times.

PART FIVE

Rich Man, Poor Man

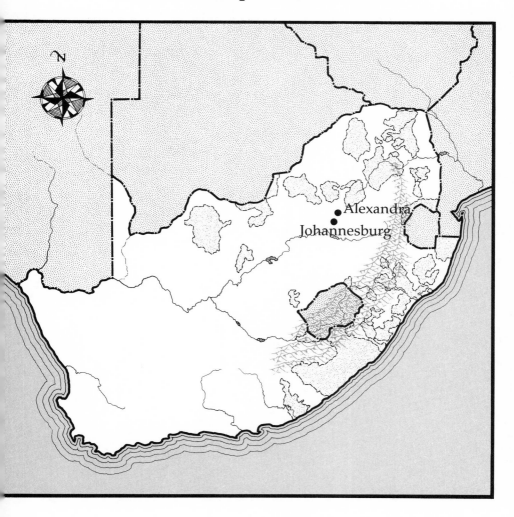

XI

JOHANNESBURG:
CITY OF GOLD

First it was diamonds. Then it was gold.
▲ ▲ ▲ ▲ ▲ The two transmuted southern Africa from a simple rural outback to a complex urban society.

This part of the story begins about 1866, when the first diamonds were found near Kimberley. The date and the details of the actual discovery vary considerably, but the boom was immediate. Fortune hunters swarmed in from all over the world to try their luck. Railroads were built from the coast to the new town of Kimberley in the northern Cape, deep in the interior. Hundreds of millions of dollars' worth of diamonds have been taken from Kimberley's Big Hole, the world's largest manmade hole, dug mostly by hand. Three skyscrapers the height of the Empire State Building could be stacked on top of one another in that hole. After the fortune hunters came the foreign investors, who put their money into what others were taking out, the diamond business.

Diamonds started the changes in South Africa, but gold kept them rolling. A century ago an Australian handyman named George Harrison picked up some interesting-looking rock on the Transvaal farm where he was working. He crushed it and borrowed a skillet from the kitchen to "pan" the gravel, washing it to separate the bits of gold from the rock. That was in 1886; it was not the first discovery of gold in South Africa, but it was the most important—the handyman's find turned out to be the biggest deposit of gold ore in the world. It came from the Witwatersrand (the Rand for short), which means "White Waters Ridge," named for the white quartzite hills that glisten in the sun after a rainstorm. Since then, 95 percent of the world's gold has come out of South African mines.

Nobody knows who "Johannes" was, but the burg that bears his name started as a patch of barren ground set aside as a camp for the diggers who came to work on the Rand. At 5,700 feet above sea level the camp grew quickly. Laid out on a grid pattern and climbing toward the sky like New York, the rock beneath it honeycombed with played-out veins of gold, Jo'burg is the biggest city in South Africa, the third largest on the continent after Cairo and Alexandria.

There is romance to gold, but that romance may be limited to the first shout of discovery and the final shaping of the precious metal into a piece of jewelry or a Krugerrand, a gold coin stamped with the image of South African leader Paul Kruger and valued by collectors. There is nothing romantic about the stages in between.

Each day hundreds of thousands of miners plunge into a network of tunnels that burrow as much as two miles below the earth's surface. Then the miners make their way to the cramped spot where they are working, perhaps far from the access shaft. With jackhammers they drill holes in the rock, pack the hole with explosives, and blast the rock free. Sweat

174

pours from the miners' bodies as they labor in the ninety-degree heat with humidity at the saturation point, despite the refrigerated air pumped constantly into the shaft. They work in constant danger, from water flooding, from rocks exploding under intense pressure, from other hazards. Most of the miners are Black; they speak a made-up language known as Fanakalo, combining Zulu, English, and Afrikaans vocabulary and developed so that miners from different language backgrounds could communicate in their work.

The rock hauled out of the mine is crushed, washed, pulverized, chemically treated, and smelted. The process is called "winning." The molten gold is poured into molds the size of a brick, containing 88 percent gold, 9 percent silver, and 3 percent impurities. When the gold is refined, the silver is separated out and most of the impurities removed to produce a bar that is 99.6 percent pure. *It takes a ton of rock to produce half an ounce of refined gold.*

Diamonds and gold are only a part of South Africa's riches. Here are the world's largest reserves of chrome, used in the production of high-grade stainless steel and best known as the shiny coating on car bumpers. Here are the largest known deposits of manganese and vanadium, both used in manufacturing steel. Uranium, platinum, iron, copper, nickel, lead, tin—the list goes on and on, earning South Africa the title of the "Saudi Arabia of Minerals." But there is a touch of irony in that title; the one thing South Africa does not have is oil.

There is plenty of coal, though; two-thirds of it used to generate electricity. Coal production paralleled the development of gold mining, with its insatiable need for power. Railroads, built to cart the diamonds out of Kimberley, were now extended to Johannesburg, connecting the gold fields of the Rand to the seaports, particularly Durban. Agriculture developed quickly to produce the maize needed to feed the hordes of people coming into the country to work in the mines. The population shifted. The Rand became the most urbanized part of the country, and someday more than half of the population of South Africa will live in the Transvaal.

Gold caused South Africa's economy to grow at a phenomenal rate, one of the fastest in the world, topped only by the United States, its largest trading partner. The problem is that now South Africa, producer of half of the world's gold, depends on the gold for continued growth and strength in the world market. But the price of gold goes up and down daily, and with it, the state of South Africa's economy.

Fluctuating gold prices are not the only problem South Africa has. Its economic health is tied not only to the price of gold but also to the country's political health. And most of the world regards South Africa's political condition as ailing badly.

South Africa has always had a hard time explaining itself and its official policies concerning everyone who is not White. People of other countries are strongly critical of apartheid. When unrest and violence inside South Africa become the focus of world attention, outside pressure increases to force the government to "dismantle apartheid." The pressure is usually economic, on the theory that when people are hurting badly enough in their pocketbooks, they will be willing to accept what had seemed before to be unacceptable change. The United States, among other measures, has prohibited the importation of the Krugerrand.

After the Peace of Vereeniging marked the end of the Second Anglo–Boer War on May 31, 1902, a new era began. In 1910 the four colonies—Cape Province, Natal, Transvaal, and the Orange Free State—became known as provinces and joined together as the Union of South Africa, a dominion of Great Britain like New Zealand, Australia, and Canada. Four areas were excluded from the Union: Basutoland, which later became Lesotho; Bechuanaland, now called Botswana; Rhodesia, renamed Zimbabwe, and Swaziland.

A fair indication of the troubles the country makers faced in putting together four provinces with sharply divided White populations—English and Afrikaner—shows up in their decision about a capital city. The English favored Cape Town, the Mother City; Afrikaners wanted Pretoria, north of Johannesburg in the Transvaal. Their solution was to make Pretoria the *administrative* capital and Cape Town the *legislative* capital. This means that every year the Pretoria government people pack up and take the overnight train down to Cape Town, where Parliament meets. When the session ends, they all pack up and go north again. And since the judicial capital also had to be somewhere, the Appellate Division of the Supreme Court was settled in Bloemfontein, in the Free State.

Tensions continued to simmer beneath the surface in the controversy over the flag. It does look as though it was designed by a committee trying to please everyone. The broad orange, white, and blue horizontal stripes duplicate the seventeenth-century flag of Holland. Centered in the white stripe are three little flags—the old Free State flag, the old Transvaal flag, and the British Union Jack sandwiched between. Introduced in 1928, it was declared the *only* national flag in 1957, and the Union Jack no longer flies officially.

The first prime minister of the new Union was a Boer general named Louis Botha (pronounced BO-tuh). Botha brought into his cabinet two other generals, Jan Christiaan Smuts and J. B. M. Hertzog, who later became prime ministers.

One of the first things the new Parliament did was to set up a Department of Native Affairs to deal with the Black population. Within a few years Hertzog started laying the foundations of apartheid. He steered the Native Land Act through Parliament, introducing the principle of setting aside land in each province for Blacks and keeping the rest for Whites. But Hertzog's intense nationalism and anti-British attitudes were too much for Botha, who forced Hertzog out of his cabinet. Undaunted, Hertzog formed the National Party, and eventually he was back in power.

The 1930s were Depression years in South Africa as they were in many other parts of the world. White farmers left their drought-stricken farms and moved to the cities to look for work. There wasn't any, or not enough. Unemployment was high; morale was low. Then in August of 1938, Afrikanerdom—that sense of national identity that is uniquely Afrikaner—surged upward. Nine ox wagons, reproductions of the original Voortrekker wagons, set out from Cape Town to reenact the Great Trek. They arrived on schedule in Pretoria on December 16, the hundredth anniversary of the Day of the Covenant. On that day they laid the cornerstone of the Voortrekker Monument on a hill outside of Pretoria. A wall encircles the ponderous building; wagons sculpted on the wall in low relief reproduce the old protective *laagers*. Inside the massive tomblike monument a sign requests silence. This surge of Afrikaner identity was crucial to its growing power and eventual control of the government by Afrikaners—not by English.

But the rest of the world was in turmoil as World War II erupted in Europe, and South Africa's attention shifted away from itself. Hertzog favored neutrality, but Smuts insisted that South Africa should enter the war on the side of the British. He ended up as advisor to Winston Churchill. Despite the strong pro-German sympathy early in the war (which was probably more *against* England than it was *for* Germany), 350,000 South Africans served in that war on the side of the Allies, including 123,000 Coloureds and Blacks. (Blacks fought Rommel's troops in North Africa with spears; Whites did not

178

trust them with guns.) South African mining engineers secretly produced uranium, a by-product of goldmining, for the first atomic bombs that helped to end the war in the Pacific, following Germany's surrender in May 1945.

The world at peace again, South African racists went back to the task of separating the races and keeping the Blacks under White domination. In the election of 1948 Daniel F. Malan of the National Party campaigned on a platform of apartheid and white domination. The "Nats" had once been a minority faction, but Malan, regarded as the architect of apartheid, had put together a platform that appealed to a majority of Afrikaners, and the National Party swept to power. It has remained in power ever since.

Malan was later succeeded by Dr. H. F. Verwoerd (fur-VOORT), who became prime minister in 1958. It was Verwoerd who transformed South Africa from a Union into a Republic, getting approval for the change by only a slim margin of the voters. Verwoerd cut all ties with the British Commonwealth. On May 31, 1961, the Republic of South Africa came into being and stood alone. Five years later Vorwoerd was assassinated, and B. J. Vorster stepped into his place. After a dozen years as prime minister, Vorster retired and took the office of state president.

Next in line was P. W. Botha, who had been minister of defense. After dealing with a scandal inherited from Vorster's administration, Botha lined himself up solidly behind the principle of multinational development (translation: shipping Blacks to homelands) and the "abolition of all unnecessary discrimination."

Botha steers a bumpy course between the reactionary right wing, which picked up a few seats in the last by-election, and the comparatively liberal Progressive Federal Party, nicknamed the "Progs," led by Dr. Frederik van Zyl Slabbert. Botha's words are usually *verligte*; when he said in a speech

179

that Whites must "change or die," he riled the *verkrampten*. But Botha is a hardliner on racial issues, very much part of the Afrikaner power structure, a member of the Broederbond and of the Dutch Reformed church, as are most Nats. His initials stand for Pieter Willem. Some people call him "Piet Wapen" (Pete the Weapon), but mostly he is referred to as "P. W."

In 1982 White South Africans voted in a new constitution, creating separate chambers of Parliament for Indians and Coloureds and approving the new position of "executive president" with its very broad powers—to choose his own cabinet, to determine which issues are to be presented to Parliament and which chamber is to deal with them, and to control a "President's Council" of sixty appointees. P. W. named himself executive state president and abolished the position of prime minister. When elections were held for the new non-White chambers, only 30 percent of the Coloured voters and 20 percent of the Indians showed up at the polls to choose their representatives in what Whites called power sharing and non-Whites call a farce, regarding the elected members as sellouts pandering to the White establishment for their own gain. Blacks do not have their own chamber of Parliament. Blacks do not vote. And if most Whites continue to have their way, they never will.

The Machinery of Apartheid in the City of Gold

Johannesburg is a high-rise city of gleaming office buildings and luxury hotels surrounded on all sides by sprawling suburbs. In one direction the suburbs are filled mainly with fine houses set in well-tended yards, many with swimming pools. The owners of these homes drive imported British and German cars to chic shopping centers. These suburbs are exclusively White. The suburbs in another direction are filled mainly with dismal houses set on unpaved streets, many sharing common water taps and outdoor privies. The renters (the residents have not been allowed to own their homes) crowd into trains and buses for the trip into the city each day to go to work. These suburbs are exclusively Black.

The residents of the White suburbs have, with rare exceptions, never seen the Black suburbs. They have no idea what life is like there. But many residents of the Black suburbs work in those White suburbs by day, returning by nightfall to their own homes. The movements of the Black residents are carefully controlled by the laws of apartheid.

Soweto, the largest Black township, actually consists of twenty-eight suburbs with roughly a million and a half inhabitants. No one knows the exact figure, because so many people are *hiding* there, living illegally, one jump ahead of the police. A policeman can demand to see a passbook at any time, and if for some reason the person fails to make the correct jump, that person lands in jail. Soweto, incidentally, is not an African word but an acronym for "SOuth WEst TOwnship." Most of the people who live there travel long distances every day by train or bus to work in the industrial complexes of the Rand or in Johannesburg or in one of the "other" suburbs with names like Rosebank, Parktown, Braamfontein.

From 1949 to this day, legislation has been continually enacted to set up the complicated machinery of apartheid and to keep it grinding. The Population Registration Act of 1950 assigns every person in South Africa to a racial group, each group to develop "in its own time and in accordance with its own predispositions." Everyone would have documents to prove what racial group they belong to; only Blacks could be called upon to prove it at any time. This law requires all Blacks over the age of sixteen to carry reference books—

domestic passports, with fingerprints and other data—with them at all times, available for police inspection. Leave it at home and you go straight to jail.

The Bantu Homelands Citizenship Act decrees that every Black South African is a citizen of one of the rural homelands, his citizenship determined by the language he speaks. The Group Areas Act of 1959, revised in 1966, determines where every racial group will live. The cities—where the money is—are exclusively for Whites. But since city Whites need Blacks to do their work, Black townships like Soweto were established by the government on the edge of White cities as "bedroom communities" for the Blacks.

But not all Blacks have permission to live even in these Black townships. A system of "influx control" laws regulates the number of Blacks who can live legally in townships near the cities; that number is determined by White need for Black labor. The rest must stay in the homelands. Blacks allowed to live in urban areas are considered "temporary sojourners." In order to be permitted to live in one of the Black townships near Johannesburg, for example, a Black must have been born in the urban area or must be able to prove that he has worked for the same employer for ten years or for different employers for a total of fifteen years. A man's eligibility for permanent residence does not apply to his wife. Unless she has fulfilled the same requirement of birth or job tenure, she is considered a "superfluous appendage." So is anyone old or sick or unable to find work. People who meet the long-term qualifications are called "Section Tenners," meaning that they have satisfied the requirements of Section Ten of the Urban Areas Consolidation Act. Being a Section Tenner is a much-yearned-for goal.

People who have not achieved Section Ten status are classified as "migrant workers." They are legally residents of the homelands, far from the cities, to which they have been assigned, but where there is no work. When they come to Johannesburg looking for jobs, they must live in hostels, huge single-sex dormitories, for eleven months of the year, going to visit their wives and children in the homelands only once a year. This yearly month-long break was formerly used as an excuse for denying Section Ten eligibility—a man could not possibly accumulate the ten or fifteen years to qualify if he went to see his family every year. This rule has now been changed to allow the annual trip home.

Many Blacks simply defy the law and live in the townships illegally, where they are constantly subject to pass-law arrest, jail sentences, and banishment back to their homeland. Or they huddle around the cities in shacks in squatter camps that are periodically bulldozed by the authorities. There have been *millions* of pass-law arrests; there will be millions more unless the system is changed. According to the South African Institute of Race Relations, which kept tabs on such statistics in 1982, 206,022 people were arrested that year for pass-law offenses, a 28-percent increase over the year before. There is no indication that the number of arrests has slackened.

The system is actually getting tighter, not looser. In 1982 new legislation was passed that reduced the time a Black without Section Ten authorization may remain in an urban area, including the Black townships. The limit went to seventeen hours, between 5 A.M. and 10 P.M.; it used to be a seventy-two-hour maximum. There are stiff penalties for harboring a curfew breaker, up to six months in jail and a fine of five hundred rand for the first offense. And there are even stiffer punishments for employing an illegal Black worker: five thousand rand and a year in jail.

This is apartheid at its most basic. It does not include what critics call the "petty apartheid" rules that are sometimes changed to make a favorable impression on visitors and on the world at large, like the "international" hotels and res-

taurants in some cities. Most theaters have been desegre-
gated, though few Blacks can afford to buy a ticket to a play,
and movie houses may apply for special status. The Main
Public Library in Johannesburg is open to Blacks as well as
Whites. White sports clubs are now admitting a few Black
members.

Many Whites resist even small advances. While I was in
Johannesburg, I read this news item: "MIXED REACTION AS
RACE BARRIERS ARE LIFTED ON ALL TRAINS. Amid much con-
fusion and little fanfare, South Africa's first mixed race trains
officially started running yesterday [September 1, 1985]. Apart
from a few carriages still reserved for Whites only, suburban
and mainline coaches are now open to all races." The mixed
reactions were from some of those the reporter interviewed.
A Post Office employee said, "Why should I sit next to a
Black? They drink too much and start trouble." Another postal
clerk said, "I don't think women will be able to travel with
their handbags anymore and the Whites-only section will be
overcrowded because all the Whites will want to sit there."
The last person interviewed said, "They get drunk and want
to fight. The next thing you know they'll want to marry our
daughters."

Opponents of Apartheid

The African National Congress (ANC), the original Black
antigovernment organization in South Africa, was founded
in 1912 on principles of nonviolence learned from Gandhi.
(Gandhi's campaign of passive resistance in Durban from
1907 to 1913, protesting discrimination against Indians, was
the first dramatic non-White protest movement in the country.) In the beginning the ANC was a conservative group
stating conservative goals: communicating to the govern-

ment of the new Union what was "uppermost in the Natives' minds." Power sharing was not a priority; complaint sharing was.

But when polite protest got them nowhere, the ANC raised the stakes. After the National Party came to power in 1948, the ANC turned to boycotts, strikes, and civil disobedience to make their point. In 1953 they adopted the "Freedom Charter," which asserts that "South Africa belongs to all who live in it, black and white," and calls for freedom and equality. It sounds something like the American Bill of Rights. That same year Chief Albert Luthuli, a teacher and Zulu leader, was elected ANC president. He was awarded the Nobel Peace Prize in 1960 for his work with the organization.

Not everyone agreed on the nonrevolutionary multiracial policies of the ANC. A faction called the Pan Africanist Congress (PAC) broke away from the original group. These two organizations were behind the pass-law protest in Sharpeville that led to the killing of sixty-seven Black protesters.

Soon after Sharpeville the government put through the Unlawful Organization Act and banned both the ANC and the PAC. Forced underground, the groups turned increasingly to violence. The ANC formed a military branch called Umkhonto we Sizwe, meaning "Spear of the Nation." Through informers the security police uncovered its secret headquarters and arrested Nelson Mandela, the underground leader.

Mandela, a British-educated lawyer descended from a family of chiefs, was arrested in 1962 and has been serving a sentence of life imprisonment since 1964. Although he is now old and sick, he still remains popular among Blacks. His wife, Winnie Mandela, was also put under government bans, restricted to a remote farm in the Free State for twenty years. It is illegal to publish Mandela's photograph in South Africa and illegal to quote him, yet something like 90 percent of the Blacks—including many who had not even been born when

185

he was sent to Robben Island—regard him as their leader. Some even predict that Mandela will be the first Black prime minister when the struggle is over, under the new regime.

P. W. Botha has offered to release Mandela if he would unconditionally renounce violence and promise not to commit any illegal acts. But Mandela refused the offer. His daughter read his statement: "What freedom am I being offered when I may be arrested on a pass offense? . . . Only free men can negotiate."

His successor in the ANC is Oliver Tambo, who heads a collective leadership from exile headquarters in Lusaka, the capital of Zambia. Many people insist that the ANC is now basically a Communist organization. Certainly there are Communists in the ANC, and Communist countries help to finance it, but Western and other African nations also provide support.

The young Blacks who were babies when Nelson Mandela went to prison were still little children when Steve Biko died. Biko was one of the leaders of the Black Consciousness Movement. Believing that Blacks had to take the initiative in their struggle for freedom, he and a group of friends left the multiracial student organization, the National Union of South African Students, that was under primarily White leadership and formed one for Blacks only. His departure upset his White friends, but he stuck to his point: Blacks and Whites needed to clean up racism in their own separate communities, and when that was done they could come together to build a multiracial South Africa. It was Biko's group that inspired the Soweto uprising in June 1976 over the use of Afrikaans in Black schools. The twenty thousand students were protesting not just instruction in Afrikaans but the total inadequacy of their schools. Violence spread throughout the country. During that sixteen-month state of emergency more than seven hundred deaths were recorded (and many more probably went unrecorded)—all of them Blacks.

One of the dead was Steve Biko. He died in September 1977 at the age of thirty-one while in the custody of the South African security police. After being beaten, denied medical treatment, and transported across the country naked and shackled, he died of brain damage. Medical examiners covered up the causes of his death, circumstances that were always officially denied until they were finally proved and made public. All of his writings and speeches are still banned.

It is always touch-and-go for Black leaders in South Africa. Allan Boesak, a Coloured minister of the Dutch Reformed church, attracted recognition through his church activities. In 1984 he helped to found the United Democratic Front (UDF), an alliance of four hundred or so organizations of all sizes, some national and some local, with a membership of about 2.5 million people. In August 1985 Boesak planned a march on the prison near Cape Town where Mandela is held to demand his release. Boesak was immediately arrested for interfering with the Internal Security Act. A few days later he was out on bail of twenty thousand rand under the following restrictions: he could not attend any meeting of more than ten people, except for church services; he could not visit schools or attend funerals without written permission; he could not leave his home from 9 P.M. to 6 A.M., and he had to report to the police station every day between 7 A.M. and 9 A.M.; he could not leave his Magisterial District except to attend court.

One of the best known and most highly visible of South Africa's Black leaders is a diminutive Anglican priest by the name of Desmond Tutu. While serving as secretary-general of the South African Council of Churches, he was awarded the Nobel Peace Prize in 1984; the following year he was elected bishop of Johannesburg. He seems like a man holding onto the reins of horses galloping in different directions. To the White horse he seems too radical, perhaps endorsing violence. To the Black horse he seems too moderate, kow-

187

towing to the Whites and avoiding the issues of violence. In an interview in *Rolling Stone* in November 1985, Tutu said, "People like me are risking the danger of rejection by our young people who say we [moderate Blacks] are standing in our [people's] way. When I said that if some of our people go on burning collaborators, I will leave South Africa with my family, some of these young people said, 'Good! Good riddance! Because you keep stopping us from finishing what we have started.'"

Tutu also says, "Our leader is Nelson Mandela."

A name that appears in the press frequently is Gatsha Buthelezi, the Zulu leader and hereditary chief who is also the elected leader of the homeland KwaZulu. Homeland leaders are generally regarded by Blacks as stooges of the White government, men who sold out to the system for their own personal gain. Sometimes Buthelezi is accused of being a sellout, too moderate, too acceptable to the Whites. On the other hand, he might also be the one who could attract a following from all the tribes and *still* be acceptable to the Whites.

He is certainly moderate. He has opposed economic sanctions against South Africa, saying it would hurt Blacks in the short run as well as the long run. He has opposed the withdrawal of American business and American investment from South Africa, claiming it would not be effective. His Zulu-based organization, Inkatha, is the largest Black movement in South Africa today. But the poll that gave 90 percent of the Blacks' backing to imprisoned Nelson Mandela gave only 6 percent of its support to Buthelezi.

There are, of course, many Whites who oppose apartheid. It is not easy for them either. One man who has suffered for his views is an Afrikaner named Beyers Naude, a "dominee," or minister, of the Dutch Reformed church who was once the most highly regarded Afrikaner clergyman, and his church one of the most prestigious in Johannesburg. His father helped found the Broederbond, and as a young man Naude became one of its members. But as a middle-aged man he left that organization to found the Christian Institute. Naude gathered around him a hand-picked group of Afrikaner ministers he hoped could quietly and gradually change the thinking of their people.

Initially as moderate as the early ANC, the Institute changed its tactics and began to advocate boycotts, sanctions, and other forms of civil disobedience. Eventually the liberal Whites who had been supporting it stopped writing checks. About the time of Steve Biko's death the organization was banned, and Naude was banned as well. For seven years it was illegal for him to travel, enter Black areas, attend meetings, or be quoted in print. In 1984, when he was sixty-eight years old, he was also "listed" in addition to being banned, an honor reserved for "dangerous security risks." (Naude is now secretary-general of the South African Council of Churches. The Dutch Reformed church is not a member of this organization.)

And then there are the women.

Its official title is the Women's Defence of the Constitution League, but its members wore black sashes at their silent demonstrations, and the organization of middle-class White women who try to help Blacks became known as the Black Sash. Formed to protest unjust laws, it emerged after the Nationalists came to power. The women used to gather wherever they knew a minister or some other powerful official was due to arrive, wearing their somber black sashes to make the official uncomfortable. The women learned that they could not stop the government but that the government could stop them. Now there are no more demonstrations, because the women are not allowed to "assemble"—not even silently. (Mary McChesney has been active in this organization in Cape Town.)

A Durban group called Women for Peaceful Change Now

planned a protest march through the center of the city to the office of the mayor to hand him a message for P. W. Botha. The chief magistrate of Durban had refused permission for the march, because the authorities would not accept responsibility for the safety of those who took part in it. Anyway, the magistrate said, waffling, it was up to the police to give permission; he could not instruct the city police to condone the march, which they believed would interfere with traffic. The police had no comment, either about responsibility for safety or interference with traffic. P. W. Botha did not get his message from the Women for Peaceful Change Now.

A Tourist in Jo'burg

The Carlton is the hotel best known to foreign travelers, as slick and posh a place as you might find in any big city, and especially in a city as prosperous as Johannesburg. It is part of the glassy, glossy Carlton Center, with its assortment of stylish shops and restaurants. One of the hotel's several restaurants is so grand that no prices are printed on the menu; presumably if you have to ask how much a meal costs, you probably can't afford to eat there anyway.

It was in that restaurant, where white-gloved waiters seemed to outnumber diners and I worried about my frontier American manners, that I had my most expensive and unusual meal in South Africa. *Warthog Fumé* the menu said in fancy script. *Fumé* means smoked, and who knew what warthog tasted like? I was a guest that evening of an educator from the United Kingdom, an Englishman enjoying the strength of the English pound against the weakness of the South African rand.

At the time I was in South Africa, the rand was worth about forty cents in U.S. currency, some days less, some days more. Six months earlier it had been double that; a year or so before that the rand and the dollar were about equal, and at one time the rand had been worth more than $1.25. The exchange rate, then, was definitely in my favor. My *Warthog Fumé*, I found out, cost R25. Had I paid for it in dollars, a luxurious meal at one of Jo'burg's finest restaurants would have cost about ten dollars.

Even the top-of-the-line Carlton Hotel might have been affordable at those exchange rates; but I was on a tight budget, so I chose to stay at a less glamorous but entirely adequate downtown hotel. No one had warned me that "downtown" meant an area of poor shops across the street from the railroad station through which tens of thousands of Blacks funneled twice each day. It was an area of beggars, some of whom displayed their mutilations or played gospel songs on accordions, and an area of thieves and muggers. One morning I came down to the lobby to find the desk clerks shaken; they had just been robbed at knifepoint, the safe emptied. Whenever I left the hotel, I arranged to be picked up at the front door by a taxi or by people who arrived with doors locked and the grim look of someone driving into the combat zone. When I decided to walk somewhere, I carried only pocket money. And when I had no other plans, I ate my meals in that hotel. That was where I learned something important about myself.

It was my first day in Johannesburg, my first day in South Africa. After a day of telephoning (even the telephones don't work like ours), making contacts, setting up appointments, asking for help, I went to the hotel lounge for afternoon tea. All of the tables were occupied, but I assumed that it was customary as it is in Europe to ask permission to take an empty seat.

At one table for four sat a snowy-haired White woman and a young Black woman (this was an "international" hotel, and more than half the people in the lounge were Black). I went to the table and asked *the White woman* for permission to sit down. It did not even occur to me to ask the Black's consent.

My omission did not dawn on me until I had placed my order. Suddenly I was acutely aware of the dark-skinned woman across the table. She ignored me. It seemed too late to apologize and maybe inappropriate too. I argued with myself that she had ignored me all along; it was the White woman who had looked up and smiled. I argued that maybe the Black woman did not speak English, although actually it was more likely that she would. The white-haired lady could have been Portuguese, for goodness' sake, except that she looked solidly English and turned out to be Australian. By the time the tea arrived I was too upset with myself to drink it. The Black woman never glanced my way.

XII

JOHANNESBURG:
CITY OF CONTRASTS

Debra and Thobeke

On my second day in Johannesburg I ▲ ▲ ▲ ▲ ▲ stopped at the Main Public Library. There were plenty of Blacks as well as Whites, which struck me as a good sign—and I was looking for good signs. The librarians had fought to keep it open to both, even when funds were cut by the government that wanted it for Whites only.

Reading rooms open off high-ceilinged halls paneled with dark wood and trimmed with polished brass. Every seat in every room was occupied by a Black student, bent over a stack of books. Rather than go in and ask who they were and what they were doing, I hung around in the hall. Finally two girls came out, one thin and primly dressed in sensible shoes and a plain cotton dress, the other one hefty, her hair done up in little braids, her clothes a raucous clash of bright colors and bold patterns.

"What are all those people doing in there?" I asked them.

The thin one covered her mouth and turned away in embarrassment, but the fat one briskly motioned me aside. "Studying," she said. "Our high schools are closed, and we have our matrics coming up soon. We want to pass our exams, so we come here to study."

I invited them to have lunch with me, and they accepted. We arranged to meet outside the reading room in an hour. I spent that hour debating where we could go to eat. I had not learned the rules yet, and although I supposed I could take them to my hotel several blocks away, I was hoping for something closer and less formal. I wondered if they would even show up.

But they did. I suggested Juicy Lucy's, a small fast-food restaurant. That seemed agreeable. We found a corner table, and while we ate hot sandwiches called Cheezas I asked questions. Debra, the bold one, answered most of them.

They told me about their homes in Pimville, one of the oldest of the Soweto townships, and about their parents and their school. The life-style they described sounded comfortable: Debra's father is an assistant to an optometrist; Thobeke's mother is the matron at a hospital. Debra has one brother and lives in an eight-room house with electricity and a telephone. Debra speaks Zulu, and Thobeke is Xhosa.

"Our school is a Catholic high school, and we got a lot of pressure from students from government high schools to boycott. It's dangerous in the township schools, so we take the train into the city every day to study in the library. It's nice and quiet there."

I asked how they felt about the boycott.

Debra said, "I just want to finish high school. Then I want to be a teacher."

"What about you, Thobeke?"

She stared at her plate and whispered, "A nurse."

"Now," Debra said, planting her plump elbows on the table, "it's your turn to answer some questions. Are you married? Do you have children? How big is your house?"

The Anglican Cathedral

Lively, energetic, high-powered Johannesburg dies on weekends. All the shops close at noon Saturday, even those in the Carlton Center. There are no museums open on Sunday, no movies, few restaurants. Jo'burg becomes a ghost town.

The Anglican Cathedral of St. Mary was just around the corner from my hotel, the street lined with beggars who made me feel guilty and assorted odd-looking characters who made me feel nervous. I went there on Saturday afternoon to find out when and where Bishop Desmond Tutu would be preaching the next day. The cathedral is a vast edifice with an ornate high altar and a lofty pulpit and rows of chairs on the stone floor. It was almost empty, but not quite. At the head of the long aisle a Black woman knelt, arms outstretched, singing an American hymn at the top of her voice:

> My faith looks up to Thee,
> Thou Lamb of Calvary,
> Saviour divine!
> Now hear me while I pray,
> Take all my guilt away. . . .

I know that hymn; I thought of singing along with her, changing her solo into a duet, but I was too self-conscious to try. Suddenly she stood up, scooped up some holy water in her hands from the font and drank it, and disappeared outside.

A crowd had gathered for the 9:15 family service at St. Martin's-on-the-Veld in Rosebank, a wealthy suburb that has not been a "veld" for a long time. Television crews set up cameras. We waited outside for the early service to let out, but it was running about half an hour late. This was Tutu's

195

first visit to this parish as bishop, and he was not going to miss an opportunity to preach.

I chatted with two women while we waited. "Most of my friends stayed away today," the first said. "We don't want Bishop Desmond coming to scold us."

"Why do you think he's going to scold you?" I asked.

"I want you to know that we are kind to everyone at this church," she answered. "*Everyone*, regardless of color. And we don't want him coming here to tell us that we're not. I very nearly stayed away myself." It was the kind of defensiveness born of guilt that is common in South Africa.

The second woman, Sue, was the friend-of-a-friend-of-a-friend from home. When I telephoned her and suggested that we meet at St. Martin's to hear Tutu, she agreed but admitted that she had serious reservations about the man. I assumed Sue was liberal; she had given me the name and phone number of a Black friend to contact in another city, a woman who had been Steve Biko's lover and had borne his child a few months after he died. (Biko's woman never returned my telephone calls; someone told me later that she was shunning publicity, probably for the sake of her eight-year-old child.)

Now the three of us, strangers to one another, stood outside what the newspaper would describe the next day as "the richest white parish of his Diocese," waiting for the bishop.

He appeared at last in full ecclesiastical regalia, a small man with a puckish grin. In the rush for seats Sue and I lost track of the other woman. There was no scolding. Tutu approached the congregation with gentle humor, acknowledging that he was not particularly welcome in that parish. The Gospel lesson that day was the story of the Good Samaritan. In his sermon the bishop turned it into a parable of love— not only the Samaritan's love for the helpless man, but the helpless man's love for the Samaritan. The man who won the Nobel Peace Prize preached love and prayed for reconciliation.

The first woman found Sue and me in the garden afterward and brought us each a cup of tea. She was beaming. "What a pity some of the people in this congregation chose not to come to hear this wonderful man," she said and rushed off to make sure he had his tea as well.

When I went back to the cathedral on a Sunday morning a few weeks later, the church was well filled, mostly with Blacks, Coloureds, and Indians; about 10 percent of the worshipers were White. The acoustics were peculiar; it was hard to hear the sermon, but the hymns rang out clearly: "Grant us courage, grant us wisdom. . . . "

The bulletin, standard means of communication in Anglican churches, listed page numbers for the service and the usual church activities for the coming week: a concert, a jumble sale (rummage sale), a religious retreat. But one item was not usual: it was a list of church members who had been detained or banned under the state of emergency. We prayed for them as we did for the sick. We prayed for the end of turmoil, for the political leaders, for the South African police and the South African Defence Force in the townships, for the youth leader of the cathedral, who was under detention, for one of the priests of the church who was awaiting trial, and for a visiting Black bishop and his ministry in the "strife-torn areas."

I was taken in hand by the greeters, turned over to the senior warden, fed chocolate cake and tea outdoors in what they called a "garden" but was actually a barren courtyard scoured by a chilly wind. St. Mary's senior warden—the highest-ranking lay person in the parish—is Coloured. Like most of the parishioners, he lived in a mixed non-White neighborhood in Johannesburg until the Soweto uprising in 1976. Then that area was declared a "black spot" and he and his family were told to get out, given a year to find a place to live in a Coloured township. Now most of the members of St. Mary's travel long distances by bus or train to attend services. They are used to it; most of them travel long distances to work as well. Some parishioners live in the suburbs, working as domestics for Whites.

The warden introduced me around, first to an American woman who had just been posted to the U.S. Embassy and complained about the hard time she was having to find affordable housing.

"What do you think?" I asked her, meaning, of course, about South Africa.

"I don't," she said. "I refuse to be drawn into it." I wondered how long she could maintain that kind of neutrality, but maybe that was the only way for an outsider to survive in the long run.

An Englishwoman talking about after-church trivia casually put her hand on my arm. When she noticed what she had done, she hastily snatched back her hand and then apologized for the haste. "Blacks see it as patronizing, when Whites touch them like that," she explained. I thought it was friendly. The rules were hard to learn.

The Englishwoman passed me along to Justin, an eighteen-year-old Black. Justin told me about his brother, James, who was in detention. Justin and James had both been studying for their matrics, but they were also planning a school boycott in their Coloured township. Two weeks earlier Justin happened to be at a church meeting when James was picked up at school by the police. If Justin had not been at the church, he would have been arrested too. Now, of course, he was worried about his brother.

After the tea and cake in the garden, the visiting bishop met with a group of people in a small chapel to talk about

198

his experiences in his strife-torn area. He opened with a joke:

"P. W. and Bishop Desmond are in a boat, and P. W. falls in. Tutu walks on water and pulls him out. P. W. returns to Pretoria and tells the press, 'The Bishop of Johannesburg cannot swim.' "

The audience enjoyed his joke at P. W.'s expense, but it was the last time anyone laughed. He described the fire bombing of his house by masked men. He described peaceful funerals where the police moved in aggressively, provoking violence by deliberately tipping over the basin of water and herbs in which mourners traditionally wash their hands at funerals. He described a scene in which buses were being overturned and set alight by teenagers. When he rushed over to stop them, he was arrested and detained as a "promoter of violence," although in fact he had been trying to stop violence.

His stories had a numbing effect. "Who fire bombed his home?" I whispered to the woman next to me. She shrugged; maybe police investigators, maybe conservative Blacks who didn't want the status quo disturbed, maybe militant Blacks for whom he seemed too moderate. No one knew—or said.

Sandra Brown

Sandra is a handsome light-skinned Coloured woman in her twenties, smartly dressed and carefully made up. She said she was involved with church youth work and wanted to talk to me. When I told her I was writing a book about teenagers in South Africa, she laughed. "There are no Black teenagers in South Africa," she said matter-of-factly. "Our children are fully adult by the time they are ten or eleven."

She offered to come to my hotel. I met her in the lobby and took her to the lounge for tea. "I don't like Whites," she informed me flatly. I thought I could handle that, maybe even deserved it. We sat at the table where I had once before rendered a Black woman invisible, and Sandra told me her story.

She grew up in the eastern Cape, the eighth of ten children. She studied theology for three years, switched to sociology, and thinks she has a chance at a scholarship to Harvard to study feminist theology. But she does not want to abandon the struggle now. Blacks always talk about "the struggle." Whites call it "the problem" or "the troubles."

Sandra talked about teenagers and the fact that there aren't any, not in the usual sense. Children of eleven and twelve have been fully politicized; most of those who have been detained are boys in their early teens. They have seized control of their political present and future, rejecting their parents' values and example of passive acceptance. " 'You got your education,' the young people are telling their parents, 'and what good has it done you? What are you doing with it?' They are saying 'NO—this has got to stop.' "

Their slogan, she said, is "Liberation Before Education," an attitude that dismays their parents, and rightly so. I pointed out that an uneducated populace leaves itself wide open to demagogues and dictators. Maybe you don't need to know math, chemistry, and great literature, but surely you need to know history? Surely you need to know how to use your own language well and perhaps other languages too?

She brushed off much of what I had to say. "The whole system is corrupt," she insisted, "and it has to be destroyed."

That was what Samuel said in Cape Town and Mrs. Ngani said in Umtata.

"What about the Communists?" I asked incautiously.

"The young people know nothing of Communism," she said. "They're not allowed to read about it or learn anything about it."

"A lot of Whites claim the Blacks are under the influence

200

of outside agitators," I said, bracing for a full blast of her scorn.

"How stupid do you think we are?" Sandra blasted. "We don't need anyone to tell us we are oppressed or what to do about it."

The police, she said, are mostly teenagers themselves, completely brainwashed and full of hatred for non-Whites, whom they have been taught to see as subhuman. She likes to taunt them: "How old are you? How many people have you killed?" She laughed, recounting scenes of her own boldness. I asked her if she was scared. "Not of the sjamboks, but of rape. The threat of rape, the intimacy of that violence—yes, that scares me. And there's a lot of it."

Sandra wants South African Blacks to identify with and band with Blacks throughout Africa. The present system separates and isolates them, and the government insists the South African Blacks are vastly better off than Blacks anywhere else in the continent. There are more than fifty independent countries in Africa and a population close to 500 million. About half of these countries have changed their names in the process of gaining independence from the European countries that colonized them.

What about tribal differences here, the contention by Whites that Blacks would not accept a leader of another tribe—a Zulu would not follow a Xhosa, for instance? (It is a contention that gained wider acceptance when bloody clashes between Zulu and Pondo, related to the Xhosa, erupted near Durban over Christmas in 1985.) Would there be conflict over that?

"Maybe for a while," she said. "Apartheid promotes those differences, and it could take a year or two for that to settle down."

Sandra, who is active at the cathedral and is employed by a church group, struggles with her Christianity. She is particularly offended by pious churchgoers—Whites—who don't want anything to change. " 'You can't push us,' the Whites say"—and I know she's right, because I heard it over and over—"you can't expect us to change overnight. We are changing at our own speed. Look how things have changed!' " Her voice is mocking.

"Have they changed at all?" I asked her.

"Very little. And whatever change there has been is the result of pressure from the United States and other countries."

Sandra is scornful of the English who pretend to sympathize with Blacks but still want to maintain control, yielding power on their own terms. But the Blacks want power on *their* terms, and they will decide how it is to be shared.

Tutu? What about him as a leader?

"Too moderate for most of us, too much within the system. The old respect for authority is dying out, and Tutu represents that authority."

We ordered a second pot of tea. Sandra glanced around the room and announced that she didn't like the look of the man at the next table, who appeared to be ignoring us but who, she said, was listening to every word. Before the tea came I tried to steer her in another direction. What about her own life, her personal goals?

"I don't have time to do much for myself," she said.

What about marriage and a family, I pressed.

"No time even to *think* about that." But then she loosened up enough to admit that she doesn't like Black South African men much better than the White ones. Black men dominate their women even more than Afrikaners do. "I'd probably try to take over in a relationship," she confessed, "and I want someone strong enough to handle that. Then we'd go on and negotiate, accepting that there is a lot in any marriage that nobody wants to do, and it gets done regardless of sex roles."

But Sandra had no intention of letting the conversation

linger on such personal matters. "Come by my office to-morrow," she said. "I have some people I want you to meet."

Sandra's smile seemed genuine when I appeared at her office door the next day. I felt as though I had been forgiven, at least temporarily, for the color of my skin. She introduced Beatrice, kneeling at the bottom drawer of a filing cabinet. "Carolyn is writing a book about South African teenagers," Sandra explained.

Beatrice kept on filing. "There are no Black teenagers in South Africa," she said.

She got up off her knees and told me about her family. Beatrice was brought up by her grandmother, who came in from the country to care for her and her brother and sisters when her father died and her mother went to work as a domestic and could no longer be at home with them. Now her own daughters, aged ten and fifteen, live with that same grandmother in another town and spend their weekends with Beatrice.

"I don't get along with my girls," she said. "I want things done in such-and-such a way, and I yell at them when it isn't done right. They never call to talk to me or ask how I am, only to ask for money," she complained. I told her American parents often have similar gripes. "Grandmother spoils them," she said. "She buys them silly things with the money I send her."

That part of Beatrice's story could have been anybody, anywhere, but the next part was strictly South African: recently her older daughter was on a hijacked bus. Bus hijacking is commonplace in the Black townships, where students either force the driver to take them where they want to go, or they drive the bus themselves. This time the girl called her mother to tell her she was safe—and not to ask for money for clothes.

Sandra took me to meet Franklin, who was working in the

office of the Detainees' Parents Support Committee, a vol-
unteer group that offers legal and psychiatric aid to detainees
and their families. Some of the detainees have been so badly
tortured that they are psychological wrecks. The office was
a madhouse of ringing phones.

Franklin is twenty-two, a quiet, serious person. He left
school at the end of Standard Six because of financial problems, but his factory job barely paid for his transportation;
there was nothing left at the end of the week with which to
help his family. Franklin was detained after a funeral in the
eastern Cape a few months earlier, but he was held for only
two weeks.

"Did they hurt you?"

"I was not tortured, but I was warned: if I become involved
in any political activity I will be detained for six months or
longer and tortured every day. Maybe killed."

I asked Franklin how the security police would know if he
were involved in a political group, such as the DPSC.

"Informers."

Franklin sympathizes with the informers, he said. "Most
of them are unemployed and desperate for some way to feed
their families. The police pay them and make them promises
in return for information about the activities of certain people." But he is not particularly worried. Like everyone else
involved in the struggle, he expects to be detained. One of
his neighbors was beaten and tortured with electric shocks
to the genitals. Franklin knows what he is in for when he is
picked up the next time.

"It's part of life," he said and answered the ringing phone.

"I am starting a rumor," Sandra said with a taunting smile
when I stopped by her office to thank her for her help.

"What's the rumor?"

"That plans are being made for the Liberation Celebration,
in 1989."

"That soon? Is it possible?"

"It's possible. Optimistic, but possible. I'll tell you what is not possible: that we hang on like this for another twenty-five years."

Rudzani

A calamity is a time of great opportunity, said the penciled note tacked to the door of Rudzani's studio.

This was beginning to look like calamity time, because Rudzani was due to fly to New York in two days for four years of study at Hunter College. But he did not yet have his papers in order. Part of the problem was that according to the South African government he is a citizen of Venda, one of the homelands recognized by South Africa but by no one else. Although he has lived all his life in Soweto, his passport says "Republic of Venda," and he was afraid the U.S. Embassy would not grant him a visa with a passport from a make-believe country. If the papers were held up too long and he missed the flight on which he was booked, the airline ticket would cost much more.

Rudzani's paintings—dramatic abstracts in vivid colors and strong vertical forms—were displayed in the front hall of the art school and stacked in his bright little studio. Rudzani is the second in his family to show an artistic gift, but his older brother has chosen not to pursue an art career. His father works for the transportation company selling bus coupons; Rudzani has seven brothers and sisters. At first his family was against his going to America, but in the end they were very proud, even though he would be far away and gone for such a long time. Maybe forever, but they didn't want to talk about that.

When I visited the art school a month later, the note

205

was gone, the door padlocked, and Rudzani safely in New York.

Lawrence

Lawrence's great love is fashion. He envies Rudzani's chance to study in America. A fifteen-year-old with big dreams, he wants to be a designer. "Someday I'll go to New York, too." Given his luck so far, that may not be an impossible dream.

His mother works as a maid for a White couple from Uganda who are virtually raising Lawrence as their son. Jeanne and her husband are sending Lawrence to an English private school, one with a less affluent student body. Lawrence's mother didn't marry his father, determined that she would never marry a South African Black. But she changed her mind recently and did marry. Black men are extremely chauvinistic and hard on their wives, Jeanne says, and Lawrence's mother is miserable. I wanted to spend more time with this interesting woman, but she was always too busy. Then a mutual acquaintance explained why: Jeanne doesn't like American women; their voices irritate her.

Lawrence's tribal affiliation is Zulu. Once a year at Christmas he visits relatives in Natal, where the women brew beer and bake biscuits like English scones. He likes it there and thinks maybe it would be better to attend school in Natal where they are on a four-term system, rather than the three-term year in Johannesburg, where stretches between breaks are longer.

Lawrence was dressed in checkered tackies, fatigues, and an argyle-patterned sweater. When I asked him questions about clothes he raced up to his room and brought out an armload of his favorites. The pants were elaborately seamed

"Triple Nines" that he said had cost him R85. A baggy pair made in France had snaps at the ankles for a close fit. He sported "professor glasses," round-lensed sunglasses with metal frames; wraparound mirrored sunglasses were once in but are now out. Pointy-toed shiny leather shoes were definitely in. He named the places teenagers shop for clothes in Johannesburg. The Saturday morning flea market is haunted by teens looking for cheap, interesting clothes.

"Wearing an outfit more than four times labels you as 'low down,' " he said.

What about drugs?

"A problem," he admitted. "Not just *dagga*"—marijuana, pronounced DAKH-ah—"alcohol too."

"Nerd" crept into the conversation regularly, a popular term for unpopular people imported to South Africa from the United States via *Revenge of the Nerds* at the local cinema. When I asked for Lawrence's definition, he described a White boy at his school, a long-distance runner who is also a bookworm.

Joshua Weiss

Joshua, who graduated last year from the University of Witwatersrand (called "Wits"—pronounced VITS) and got a job in England, took me to meet his parents in Norwood. On the way to this Jewish suburb (Jo'burg Whites group themselves ethnically in their suburbs), he told me his family's story. After his mother died a few years ago, his father, Stanley, remarried. His stepmother Ruth had returned to South Africa after living in Israel for nearly twenty years. It took her a while to adjust to Stanley's family of grown-up children, especially when it came to cooking for holidays.

"At first Ruth served mostly cucumbers and cottage cheese,

but now she's been taking cooking lessons. It will be a feast."

And it was. Stanley's look-alike brother Ned and his wife Natalie were also there. Stanley and Ned maintained a brooding silence while the two women chattered ebulliently and the food emerged from the kitchen in a steady parade of heaping bowls and platters. The dinner came to a grand finale with rum-flavored orange mousse; chocolate cake was served with coffee later in the evening. The conversation was mostly about South Africa and how to leave it.

"Twenty years in Israel, through all the violence there, but I was never as frightened in Jerusalem as I am in Johannesburg," Ruth said. "All they have to do is come over that hill, and they're right in our front yard." The front yard had a new townhouse with a Mercedes parked in the driveway. "They," of course, are Blacks.

But Stanley was sanguine. "Everything will get sorted out," he said, minimizing his wife's fears.

I had seen a newspaper article headlined: "QUALIFICATIONS YOU NEED FOR 'CHICKEN RUN.' " It was a summary of the basic requirements for emigration to five countries: the United States, Australia, Britain, Canada, and Israel. In ten months in 1984 nearly three thousand people left South Africa, an increase of 20 percent over the same period the year before, most of them bound for Britain. Jews in South Africa are in a better position than most others; if they want to emigrate to Israel, they will be admitted, no questions asked. South African immigrants in Israel are often dubbed "VVs" (villas and Volvos) because of the preferential treatment they receive. If Stanley is wrong, the Weisses have an option.

Ruth wants to go now, before it gets any worse. Joshua had already worked out his answers: when his leave ended he would go back to a job with a retail chain based in London. But there was no indication that Ruth would be able to talk

Stanley into going to Israel, as long as he believes everything will "get sorted out"—meaning that the Whites stay in control.

"Episodes of an Easter Rising"

The puppeteers, two men and two women, bent tenderly over their marionettes and brought them to life. The puppets were about two feet tall, their heads and hands disproportionately large. The stage setting was sparse, three doll-sized chairs and a table, no decoration, no background.

Handspring Puppet Company was founded in 1981 with the idea of establishing a repertoire of South African plays for South African children. For the first few years they were content to use puppetry as an educational medium, taking their play about dental hygiene around the country and developing a presentation about the human heart. Then they ventured into adult puppet theater with "Episodes of an Easter Rising." The performance was held at a small theater in the complex at Wits, the university known for its liberal leanings. I talked to a woman in the lobby before the play. "It's good to see these things," she said. "It shows you what the avant garde is thinking, the direction of the thrust." She was going to see a Shakespeare comedy.

"Episodes" is about two women on an isolated farm on the veld. The women shelter a Black man who appeared on their farm wearing two-tone sport shoes. The local police inspector tries to persuade the women to tell him about the Black man, claiming the man has caused trouble in a factory in the village. The inspector asks the women to release a pigeon if the man returns, a second pigeon if he leaves again. In flashback the women recall the arrival of the Black man and realize that the man they are sheltering was wounded by a bullet, not by a spear as he had told them. They stay with him until he dies; after they bury him they release the two birds. But the inspector takes them to the hospital to identify a body. Lying on a gurney, the two-tone sport shoes dangling at his feet, it seems to be the same man. Or maybe not.

Throughout the performance my attention shifted between the characters and the puppeteers hovering above them. Dressed in black and speaking with almost musical voices, the puppeteers were a presence in themselves. When a puppet reached for a glass of water, it was the puppeteer's hand—not a string—that helped it to lift the glass. The release of the two birds was performed like a dance. The audience was left in a hush of mystery.

"Episodes" was written by a South African playwright living in England, David Lytton. South Africa has several notable playwrights and novelists worth paying attention to. The playwright best known outside the country is Athol Fugard, whose 1982 play set in the 1950s, "Master Harold" . . . and the boys has been performed on public television and by repertory theater companies around the United States. Paul Slabolepszy's provocative and entertaining plays are regularly performed at the Market Theatre in Johannesburg. I missed "Slab's" newest play but saw instead a docu-drama titled Born in the RSA, researched and created by the actors themselves. (Authors Alan Paton and Nadine Gordimer may have a larger following outside South Africa than they do in the country they love but criticize in their work. Most South Africans I met suggested I read the enormously popular books of adventure-story writer Wilbur Smith, who has created a sort of Zimbabwean James Bond.)

The Market, once the city's main fresh-produce market converted into several performance spaces, is within a couple of blocks of John Vorster Square and the infamous police headquarters where detainees are routinely tortured. Born in *the RSA* was about police torture, narrated in harrowing detail by seven characters who included a White spy, a Black trade unionist, and a civil-rights lawyer. In a country known for its strict censorship, the subject matter was a shock. Who let it pass? I heard several explanations: One is that playwrights of controversial material keep censors at bay by providing them with continual rewrites, none of which will pass, all the while keeping the play going. By the time the censors are ready to close it down, the play has completed its run. The man who directs the Market says censorship is no longer functioning in city theaters, but you can't take a play to the townships. The other explanation is that there is no logic to censorship.

Prudence Meredith

The first thing I learned about this woman with charcoal black eyebrows and a dry sense of humor was that her parents had given her a completely inappropriate name. Prudence is anything but prudent, possibly one of the most outspoken people I met in my weeks in South Africa. (I learned later that she was a member of Black Sash and that the Merediths' phone had been periodically tapped. I also knew that she had been fired from one job for being overly critical of governmental racial policy.) Each time I stopped in Johannesburg before taking off in another direction, I called Prudence. Through her I met others. She advised me on plays to see, people to call, places to visit. She and her husband, Gregory, took me home to a house previously owned by a flamboyant artist with a penchant for brilliant colors. Pru and Gregory decided that painting white over purple ceilings and orange walls was too expensive; they would live with it for a while. They have lived with it now for half a dozen years.

Prudence teaches in a school for girls and invited me to

211

spend the day there. The school enrolls about six hundred pupils, a third of them boarding students from outside of Johannesburg. Unlike the private school in Grahamstown that receives a government subsidy, this school is privately funded. And expensive. There was a scant handful of Black students.

The headmistress is a feisty woman who had yanked the debating club out of a meet with a school that proposed to argue the question, "Is Bishop Desmond a Warmonger?" Her girls were dismayed; after all, they intended to take the *negative* side.

"It's not a debatable issue," she told them, and that was the end of the discussion.

On the way to the first class I glimpsed through the open door of the washroom dozens of white panama hats hanging on pegs and lined up on shelves above the sinks. The hatless girls wore perky blue-and-white-checked dresses. When the Standard Four girls sat crosslegged on the floor of the library I noticed that they wore blue underpants as well. The first thing they did, those bright-eyed, pink-cheeked eleven-year-olds in little-girl dresses, was to point out that I was mispronouncing the one phrase of Afrikaans I thought I had mastered.

Fresh from a conversation with a cab driver who complained about his problems with his maid, I brought up the subject of servants. All the girls had them at home—including the one Black child in the class.

A second group wanted to meet outside in the spring sunshine, where we talked about "sport." "Is it true," one of them asked me, "that in the United States schoolchildren actually study tennis as a subject, like maths or history?"

Like their Afrikaner counterparts, English students view American students as academic dilettantes who get away with an embarrassing minimum of course requirements and

212

discipline. In this school as in most others, sport is required but is not part of the curriculum, so that everybody is busy after classes with some sort of physical activity. I asked if the emphasis on sport produces competitiveness, but one of the girls reassured me, "That's only true among those who are very good at it, and most of us are not."

Fortified with tea and tiny sandwiches that appeared in the teachers' lounge, I went off to meet the "upper school" girls. Word had gone out that an American writer was around, and forty high school students jammed into the library to pommel me with questions. There was nothing shy about these young women; I wondered if they would behave the same forthright way in the presence of boys, or if they would shrink into silence like the Afrikaner girls.

The accent of one girl intrigued me; it sounded like a strange mixture. And so it was. Jennifer Wright turned out to be an exchange student from Texas, but in her few months in South Africa she had picked up a veneer of clipped South African tones that thinly masked her native drawl.

The attitudes and opinions of the girls turned out to be more conservative than I expected, echoing the attitudes and opinions of their parents rather than those of some of their teachers. When I asked what they thought of Bishop Desmond, who happened to be on the board of their school, they told me he should stay out of politics. "Priests have no business meddling in people's lives."

Then they switched to the subject of America and American ways. Once more I was instructed on the importance of wearing uniforms. (I did not disagree, and neither did Jennifer.) They assume that most American teenagers are high on marijuana most of the time. "Don't South African kids smoke dagga too?" I asked them. They admitted that some do. Under further pressure they also admitted that drugs and alcohol are more prevalent in the cities than in the country. I said I thought that's the way it was in America, too.

They were plainly distressed about their own image abroad. "Why do American teenagers hate us so much?" a girl named Mary cried out.

The question rocked me. "They don't hate you," I said, but I did not drop it there. "I don't want to disappoint you, but I doubt that most American teenagers give much thought to you and your problems and your political situation. I don't think most American teenagers know much about South Africa. That's why I'm writing this book—so they'll know more than they do now."

By the time this book is published, Mary will have been in the United States for several months as an exchange student. She will have arrived here braced for hostility that I would bet she hasn't found. Curiosity, perhaps—I hope so —but not hatred. She was not willing to believe that then.

Next they were deeply into their resentment of "the world" telling South Africa what to do. I had heard that one too many times, and by then I was both bored and irritated by it. I said I thought the world, including the United States, feels it has the right to speak out against what it sees as an evil system.

"I don't think you realize the sheltered little space you live in," I said. "It's like a glass bubble, protecting you from misery and violence only a few miles from where we're sitting."

The teacher interrupted. "The world wants to shatter our bubble instead of letting us break it ourselves."

"There's not that much wrong here," Mary insisted. "And besides, things are changing."

The glass bubble had apparently protected Mary and her classmates from the current focus of conversation in the teachers' lounge. An Anglican church nearby had been tutoring Black students scheduled to write their matrics in six weeks. The day before, a neighbor had complained to the police about Blacks in a White area. The police responded with typical brutality. Some of the students were standing outside the church on a break; the police interpreted this as "unlawful assembly" and rushed in, swinging their sjamboks, detaining as many as they could grab. No one returned to the tutoring classes at the church.

Priscilla Chambers

"Would you like to come to a place where we really discuss the problems of South Africa?" Priscilla whispered. She followed me as I left the library and wrote down the address of the church where her youth group was meeting that night. I promised to meet her there.

Jo'burg cab drivers were not good at finding Anglican churches. As usual this one drove in expensive circles until he finally blundered on the church where, on a typical Friday night, as many as seventy young people turn up to sing, meditate on Christian themes, share personal religious experiences, and—when the Holy Spirit is present—speak in tongues, a spiritual gift mentioned in the Bible in which people utter a language intelligible only to those who have the spiritual gift of understanding.

Priscilla was not there yet, but it was the kind of group where no introduction was needed. Forty or so teenagers and a handful of adults had been greeting each other with hugs. Then with guitar accompaniment they began singing songs of the Christian charismatic renewal movement. I sat in the back row where I could spot Priscilla when she arrived and sang along.

A dark-haired boy of about eighteen stood up to lead the meditation. He talked about Elijah, the Old Testament prophet, who had been depressed and wanted to give up. "But we

215

must not get discouraged," the speaker said earnestly. "We have to turn everything over to the Lord, not just part of our lives but everything, and He'll make it right." He talked then about "the problems, the very bad time the country is going through." And he urged his listeners to "change yourselves on the inside, and the outside will change as well."

Priscilla, dashing in late from her karate class, later explained that she prefers to spend her Friday nights at the youth meeting, rather than going out partying. "It's much more fun here," she said, "but most of my classmates don't understand that." When we paired off for sharing time, we were instructed to tell our partners about our special gifts. Priscilla told me she had learned to share her faith with others in her group at school who claim not to be interested in religion. This was a breakthrough for her. "I've never been able to talk about it before, and my friends were willing to listen."

At the coffee break I spoke with John, a man in his thirties who had moved his family to Johannesburg from London several years ago. His business had been successful, and he was now able to spend one full day a week doing "the Lord's work." In the church kitchen over instant coffee we got into the usual topics. John's wife reacted to my query about Bishop Desmond with the standard, "I just wish he'd keep his mouth shut."

"Apartheid is a mold, a matrix," John said. "You can take the mold apart but the shape will remain."

"It can't be done overnight," someone added, joining the conversation. "There have already been enormous changes," someone else put in. "We need more time. You can't rush us."

Priscilla had promised that I would hear something different in this church group, but when the singing and praying stopped, I heard the same old things one more time.

Kevin Connell

"Two years, that's 730 days," Kevin said, "and I have done 409 of them, leaving 321."

Kevin was answering my questions about military service, compulsory for all White males who must put in two years of active duty followed by a reserve requirement that lasts for a dozen more years. After Kevin gets through the rest of his active duty, he will still be on call for one-month or three-month periods on alternating years through six cycles, a system that plays havoc with careers, interrupting a man's work for as long as ninety days every other year.

But according to Kevin, a tall man of twenty-three with curly blond hair and a nonstop smile, the army is enormously fair. The South African Defence Force (SADF), as it is known, is 92 percent White. Blacks are not drafted, and the few in the force are career men. There is no discrimination in terms of pay or status. The official language alternates monthly between English and Afrikaans; he says he has no problem with the Afrikaners.

Although Kevin seems not to be doing badly with army life—his weekends are free to return to Johannesburg to see his girlfriend and attend the Friday night youth group—he has had some profound philosophical problems with the SADF. "I object to the Defence Force being used to back up the police, a group that seems to have turned crazy and vicious. They overreact in virtually all situations." When Kevin realized he would have to carry a rifle, he prayed long and hard. "I have a lot of Coloured friends," he said, "and I could not bear the idea of being ordered to shoot one of them. This is not defense of my country, the way I see it."

Kevin considered going through an expensive legal procedure to have himself declared a conscientious objector. (Despite recent legislation, COs are often imprisoned, several hundred in the past few years.) His decision, like all the important ones in his life, was made because of his relationship with the Lord. Somehow, he managed to have himself reassigned. Now he works with computers at a base not far from Johannesburg and no longer has to carry a rifle. And he has only 321 days to go.

Jennifer Wright

Jennifer, the girl with the Texas accent filtered through South African, extended an invitation for my last night in South Africa: to attend a Rotary meeting with her. And so I ate liver and onions, perhaps my least favorite meal, and sat shrouded in the smoke of innumerable cigarettes and cigars, listening to speeches and the kind of business such men's groups thrive on. It seemed dull to me, but Jennifer is obviously their darling. She is pretty, smart, bouncy, outgoing. She wants to be a lawyer. The Rotarians of her Texas town could not have chosen a better ambassador; she presents a picture of all that is good and wholesome about American youth, and they love her in Johannesburg. Her habit of announcing at the end of a full meal, "I'm stuffed," drives them wild; "stuffed" has a sexual connotation and is never used in polite company. She still sometimes forgets and says it anyway.

Driving back to my hotel with her sponsor, a businessman, I asked Jennifer if she was getting a chance to see much of the country. She said she was, with trips to Durban, to Cape Town, to Kruger National Park to watch the animals. "That's the *real* South Africa," she told me, meaning the game preserve.

"Are you meeting many Blacks?" I asked her.

Pause. "Well—the maids."

"Besides the maids?" I persisted.

Her host interrupted. "There is no reason for Jennifer to meet Blacks," he said flatly. "She has nothing in common with any of them, and there would be nothing to talk about."

It will be an interesting view of South Africa that Jennifer takes home to Texas. She will know more about the elephants of Kruger than she will about more than 70 percent of the population of the country where she will have spent a year "learning about the people."

ALEXANDRA

▲ ▲ ▲ ▲ ▲ **G**ive it a miss. It's too dangerous to go out to the townships now."

But I really did not know how I could write a book about South Africa if I had not at least *seen* one of the Black townships on the edge of Johannesburg. There was a time when buses took foreign visitors on a carefully plotted tour of Soweto that included a stop at a park given many years ago to the Blacks of the city by a wealthy mining magnate. The catch was that Blacks were barred from entering the park; only people who arrived on tour buses were allowed in. Later the ban was lifted and another requirement put down in its place: admission was five rands. For some Soweto residents that could be half a month's rent money.

Before the state of emergency declared in July 1985, Whites were required to apply in advance to the proper (White) agency to get into Soweto. But when I was in Johannesburg, few Whites were going to Soweto, those who went did not bother with paperwork. And none of them would take me. A glance at the headlines explained why no one wanted to be responsible for my safety, and I did not want to endanger anyone else. My best bet was to go with a Black who was known in the area, and I had no candidates. With the wrong person, someone not trusted, we would both be in trouble. I asked my friend Pru Meredith to work on it.

Friday was to be my last day in South Africa. Early that morning I was awakened by a phone call from a friend of Pru's. "Friday is absolutely the worst day," he said. "Fridays they search all the cars coming into Soweto to make sure nobody's violating the boycott of White shops and bringing in goods from outside. If they see a White woman, it's tickets for you."

I thanked the caller, rolled over, and went back to sleep.

At the earliest reasonable hour I called Pru. "Any more ideas?"

"Pitch up here after lunch," she said. "Bishop Desmond is coming to give First Communion to some of our little girls. A few parents are refusing to let their darlings receive the holy wafer from Black hands."

She knew how angry this would make me. But it would be the last time I had to keep from shooting off my mouth in South Africa. At seven o'clock that evening I would be on the plane for New York.

I spent the morning playing tourist. I bought an elephant-hair bracelet which the salesman promised would bring me luck. I packed my bags and checked out. Then I took a taxi to Pru's school. Prudence met me, grinning.

"You're going to the township. Father Taylor will be here for you at two o'clock."

"Soweto?"

"Alexandra. A smaller one. His church is there. He says that no one harms him, and no one will harm his friend."

There was no time to get anxious about this. Father Taylor,

a round, hearty man, bounded in with a clumsy puppy under his arm. Its name was George, and it seemed much too small for its skin. Minutes later George was huddled in the back seat, and we were on our way.

Alexandra, on a compass point exactly opposite Soweto but closer to the heart of Johannesburg, nestled among White suburbs, recently "celebrated"—if that can be the word—seventy years of existence. It occupies one square mile with a resident population of about 200,000, only some 80,000 of whom are legal Section Tenners. The streets are unpaved and deeply rutted. Rivers of rubbish flow along both sides of the street, occasionally scooped up by a trash remover.

There are gaps between the buildings like missing teeth, open spaces covered with rubble. Solid-looking brick dwellings are fenced in with sheets of corrugated metal or whatever can be found as a deterrent to thieves. Everywhere are shacks built behind shacks, an outdoor privy to serve several families, one water tap per block.

Little boys roll a hoop made from a bicycle wheel. Women in brilliantly colored clothes, hips heavily padded in the style of their country tribe, carry loads on their heads and babies on their backs. People make money selling whatever they can, hawking live chickens or heaps of vegetables along the streets or in a marketplace. Young people hang around who should be in school, if schools were open. Men hang around who should be working, if there were jobs.

But even in this small area there are "haves" as well as "have-nots," a tiny part of town with paved streets and houses that might be in a pleasant middle-class suburb. Nearby is an area of new government-built houses available at enormous rents. In a third part of town Father Taylor pointed out what he calls "the greatest iniquity," the men's and women's hostels, huge single-sex dormitories that resemble prisons.

"Only South Africa legislates that men cannot live with their families and sleep with their wives," he said, referring to laws that assign people to homelands and limit who may live in the cities. "These migrants have the same needs as any married men. The permanent residents dislike them because they use local women sexually. And many local women are willing to sell their bodies as the only way they have to make money."

The high school is shut, many of its windows smashed. There are several burned-out buildings; one is the former home of the mayor, a roofless gutted house with only four scorched walls still standing, next door to the Dutch Reformed church, which is untouched. The mayor, who is also the *dominee* of the church, is considered a collaborator with the government. The man is undoubtedly lucky to have lost only his home. Businesses owned by Whites and by members of the government-controlled "council" have also been petrol-bombed and destroyed. A few may actually be trying to help, Father Taylor said, but most are in it for what they can get. What they have been getting is trouble.

In this one square mile with its dense population Taylor has counted 102 churches, sometimes just a tumbledown shanty with a cross teetering above the door. One of the ways Blacks have found to exercise leadership without interference from Whites is to create their own churches and invent their own ways to worship.

Taylor, a recovered alcoholic, deplores the effect drinking has had on his township and on his people. He despises the bottle shops, the illegal shebeens. "Drink is the biggest curse of my people," he said. We drove past a beer hall where men hung around, unemployed men with nowhere to go but here and nothing to do but get drunk to dull the pain of their lives.

We stopped a couple of times on this unofficial tour, once

near a market area beneath a large billboard showing a happy Black man pouring a glass of Castle beer under the headline "When You're Feeling Good about Feeling Good." Makeshift tables were put together from battered oil drums and squares of plywood, some sheltered by tattered garden umbrellas. There were a lot of people but not much business. "I won't be gone long," Father Taylor said and disappeared into a house, leaving me alone.

In another country I might have gotten out to wander around this pathetic market, but I stayed in the car. People stared. I wondered where Father Taylor had gone and when he would come back. I hoped people would recognize his car as they recognized his cherubic face above the clerical collar and cross. Then I heard his voice—thank God!—and he climbed back in the car, laughing.

"Nervous?"

"Yes."

"Hostile stares?"

"Mostly curious. I think."

We stopped briefly at Father Taylor's home, a neat house with a neat yard surrounded by a tough chain link fence topped with loops of barbed wire. A woman came out to collect George from the back seat and to turn him loose in the yard with his father, a mean-looking, heavy-bodied animal that glowered through the fence. No one has yet harmed Father Taylor or his friends, but his property is not safe. "It's the incredible poverty," he said. "Sometimes the only way to survive here is to steal from others."

A few doors away is a youth center, where youngsters were getting ready for the anniversary of the center as well as for the celebration of the church's saint's day on September 29, the Feast of St. Michael and All Angels. Under the supervision of a youth leader the children had cut out circles of white cardboard and lettered on it "WELCOME TO THABI-

SONG. 25TH ANNIVESARY" (misspelled). They were stapling little ribbons of blue crepe paper to the badges, and they gave me one to pin on my shirt.

The church across the street bakes under a corrugated metal roof. The plaster crumbles from the brick, and a film of dust coats the pews. The congregation consists of about five hundred families. It has not been easy to build a congregation from a hostile, suspicious neighborhood, but Father Taylor did it, he said, "with love."

"All you can do is love them. I preach a gospel of reconciliation. 'We are the reconcilers,' I tell them. 'It's up to us.' I offer my people the love of God as an alternative to the hopelessness and despair that drive them to drunkenness and violence."

It is an unremarkable church, with a single striking exception: at the front of the church is a large hymn board with five columns of numbers. Most Anglican churches have only one column, listing four or five hymns to be sung during the service. But these columns are headed ZULU, XHOSA, TSWANA, SOTHO, and A&M (the English-language hymnal of the Anglican Church, titled "Ancient and Modern"). At Sunday morning services the worshipers sing the same hymn tune, but each sings in his or her own language. Five languages. It seemed the perfect metaphor for what South Africa could be: all the disparate groups singing together, in their own language, but the same tune. I wished I could be there to hear it.

A bronze plaque lists the names of White corporations and civic leaders who sponsor the Community Center of Alexandra. The handsome brick building is well maintained and well equipped. There is a computer room, a darkroom, a typing room with new electric typewriters all donated by IBM, a kitchen (Taylor objected to an improbable poster illustrating the proper wines to serve with different kinds of

225

food, telling the woman in charge, "We don't need to be told to drink *anything!*"). I felt as though I had just stepped into a different world—a world where things were neat and safe and attractive, exactly the opposite of everything around it. I suspect that it was created by "guilt money," donated by the people who benefit most from the system that creates the poverty and destitution in the first place. Nevertheless, the center exists.

Moses was working in the art room on the first floor. A slim seventeen-year-old in cutoffs, tackies, and a white shirt open to the waist, he showed me the giant chess pieces, the masks, the clay figures that the boys there had made. And then proudly he wheeled out his own creation. It was a wire sculpture, a folk-art form popular in the rural areas, where children run along the road pushing wire toys at the end of a rod. Moses had constructed a complicated trailer truck of elaborately manipulated wire. The truck was nearly three feet long, rolling smoothly on old tennis balls.

Moses' truck was quite sophisticated, almost beautiful. It had taken two weeks of work, of bending and shaping and soldering. Two weeks that he was not in school. Two weeks that he was not stoning cars or robbing houses. Somehow against all odds a young Black man ("There are no Black teenagers in South Africa") had turned his back on the ugliness of his world and created something to be proud of.

▲ ▲ ▲ ▲ ▲ ▲
EPILOGUE

▲ ▲ ▲ ▲ ▲   I cried when I left South Africa. I cried because it is a rich and beautiful country torn by strife, fearful Whites on one side, angry Blacks on the other. And I don't know if there is enough compassion and goodwill to triumph over misunderstanding, stubbornness, and greed and to prevent the disaster that seems inevitable. I had met dozens of South Africans, become close to a few of them, liked them even when I disagreed with them. When their lives touched mine, my life was changed; maybe theirs were too. When I left, I knew that I would never see most of those people again. But I will not forget them.

I'll remember Samuel Mkunqwana in Cape Town, disappointed in the results of the school boycott. Mary McChesney, working for change and recognizing that if it comes she stands to lose much of what she has. Marianne du Plessis, blaming the riots on the hooligans, and Marianne's maid, Tillie, trying to protect her only son from political involvement.

I'll remember Ahmed Kumar, holding out against government pressure to keep his family's home. Kaya and Paul, waiting for Jesus while bombs are planted at their university. Christie van Wyck, asking if I have a "magical solution" for his country's problems. Kevin Connell, counting the days he has left in the Army.

I'll remember Black students singing in their classroom and Black farm girls preparing for their initiation rites. Koos and Edna van der Merwe, explaining and explaining their point of view. Hennie Potgieter, assigning Blacks to a low point on the evolutionary scale. Fitzhugh McCarthy, who can't bear to leave Africa and can't bear to be there.

I'll remember Geoff and Carol Cooper, who cherish their school traditions. Mr. Peterson, wanting to increase Black enrollment in his school, and the regal Mrs. Ngani, dreaming of a school for Black children that will give them a "White" education.

I'll remember Jean Roussouw, glaring over his brandy glass and calling me a "bloody Yank" and his cook a "bloody Kaffir" while his wife does what she can to help the Blacks she employs.

I'll remember the ragged tennis players at the school in the Ngqeleni kraal and Lawrence collecting trendy clothes in Jo'burg. Sandra Brown planning a Liberation Celebration, and Prudence Meredith speaking her mind.

I'll remember Rudzani on his way to study in New York, and Jennifer Wright, the exchange student from Texas, and her skewed image of South Africa in which she knows no Blacks.

And as my plane climbed above Johannesburg and headed west toward the sunset, I knew finally that I would never forget Moses and his graceful wire sculpture.

You see things as they are and ask "Why?"
But I dream things that never were and ask "Why not?"

228

▲▲▲▲▲▲
GLOSSARY

(Pronunciation guide to names and foreign phrases)

Afrikaans [ah-frih-KAHNZ]—derivative of Dutch language
    spoken by Afrikaners
Afrikaners [ah-frih-KAHN-erz]—descendants of Dutch,
    German, and French settlers in South Africa
apartheid [ah-PAHR-tayt]—meaning "separateness";
    system of racial segregation
assegai [ASS-eh-gy]—spear used by Black tribesmen
baas [BAHS]—master or boss
bafana [bah-FAH-nah]—Black teenage boy
bakkie—pickup truck
Bantu—collective name for Black languages of southern
    Africa; meaning "the people," it now has derogatory
    connotations
biltong [BIL-tahng]—beef or other meat cured by sun
    drying

Bloemfontein [BLOOHM-fahn-tayn]—capital of Orange
    Free State
bobotie [boh-BOH-tee]—curried beef dish
boer [BOOHR]—farmer; Afrikaner
boerewors [BOOHR-wurs]—sausage
Bophuthatswana [BOH-pooh-taht-SWAH-nah]—homeland
    for Tswana, north of Johannesburg; site of Sun City
braaivleis [BRY-flays]—South African barbecue
Broederbond [BROOH-der-bahnd]—powerful
    "brotherhood" organized to promote Afrikaner
    supremacy
Casspir—armored vehicle used by South African police
Ciskei [SIHS-ky]—Black homeland near Kei River
dagga [DAKH-ah]—marijuana
dominee—minister of Dutch Reformed church; also known
    as *predikant*
hoerskool [HOOHR-skohl]—high school
Huguenots [HYOO-geh-nahts; HYOO-geh-nohz]—French
    Protestants, among first European settlers in
    Southern Africa
jonkershuis [YONK-erz-hays]—"young man's house,"
    where adolescent Afrikaner boys live
Kaffir—derogatory name for Blacks; battles between White
    and Black cattlemen in eighteenth century are
    known as the Kaffir Wars
Karoo [kah-ROOH]—vast dry area occupying about one-
    third of South Africa's land surface
Khoisan [KOY-sahn]—brown-skinned aborigines of
    southern Africa
koeksisters [KOOHK-sis-terz]—fried dough dipped in honey
koppies [KOP-eez]—flat-topped sandstone ridges
kraal [KRAHL]—village of thatched mud huts
laager [LAH-ger]—circle of wagons used by Voortrekkers
    as protection against attacking Black tribesmen;

symbol of closed thinking characteristic of
conservative Afrikaners

lobola [loh-BOH-lah]—price paid by husband to his bride's
family

lorry—English word for large truck

matrics—matriculation examinations taken by students in
final year of high school; also, students preparing for
these exams

mealies—corn; maize

mealie-lands—cornfields

mealie pap—hominy

motolo [moh-TOH-loh]—apron worn by girls to cover
genitals and indicate readiness for marriage

Natal [nah-TAL]—smallest of four provinces of South
Africa

Nederduitse Gereformeerd Kerk [NAY-der-dayt-seh kheh-
re-FOR-myert KEHRK]—Dutch Reformed church;
also called NGK

predikant [PREH-dih-kahnt]—minister of Dutch Reformed
church; also called *dominee*

Rand—short for Witwatersrand; also, unit of South
African currency

rondavel [rahn-DAH-vel]—round mud hut with conical
thatched roof

sjambok [SHAM-bahk]—hard leather whip

sosatie [soh-SAH-tee]—spicy chunks of grilled lamb

Sotho [SOO-too]—Black tribe of South Africa

Soweto [so-WEH-to]—Black township adjacent to
Johannesburg

spruit [SPRAYT]—Afrikaans for freshwater spring

stoep [STOOHP]—long front porch characteristic of Cape
Dutch architecture

technikon [TEK-nih-kahn]—technical school on university
level

Transkei [TRAHN-sky]—homeland for Xhosa and Sotho, along Indian Ocean

trek—Afrikaans word meaning "slow, arduous journey"

trekboers [TREK-boohrz]—"wandering farmers"; early settlers of southern Africa who searched out new grazing lands

tsotsis [SAHT-seez]—Black hooligans who terrorize Black neighborhoods

Tswana [TSWAH-nah]—Black tribe of South Africa

Umkhonto we Sizwe [oohm-KAHN-toh weh SIHZ-weh]— "Spear of the Nation"; military branch of the African National Congress

Umtata [oohm-TAH-tuh]—capital of Transkei

veld [FELT]—field or open place

Venda [VEN-da]—Black tribe of southern Africa

verkrampten [fayr-KRAHMP-tehn]—hard-line conservative Afrikaners who oppose any change in apartheid system

verligte [fayr-LIKH-tehn]—enlightened Afrikaners who support change in apartheid system

vetkoeks [FEHT-koohks]—fried dough filled with butter and cinnamon

volkskool [FOLK-skol]—elementary school

Voortrekkers [FOR-trek-erz]—thousands of people who left the Cape Colony in 1834 in search of new homes, free of British domination

Witwatersrand [vit-VAH-terz-rand]—rich gold-bearing ridges near Johannesburg

Xhosa [KOH-suh]—Black tribe of southern Africa

Zimbabwe—country to the north of South Africa, formerly known as Rhodesia

Zulu—Black tribe of southern Africa

▲▲▲▲▲▲
FURTHER READING

Africa: The People and Politics of an Emerging Continent. Sanford J. Ungar (New York: Simon and Schuster, 1985)

Move Your Shadow. Joseph Lelyveld (New York: Times Books, 1985)

Waiting: The Whites of South Africa. Vincent Crapanzano (New York: Random House, 1985)

Part of My Soul Went with Him. Winnie Mandela (New York: W. W. Norton, 1984)

INDEX